Organize or Agonize

LARRY AIKENS

Published by

Spark of Grace Ministries
Williamsport, Maryland

Organize or Agonize
© 2001 by
Larry G. Aikens, Jr.

All rights reserved. No part of this book may be reproduced in any form without permission in writing from the publisher, except in the case of brief quotations embodied in critical articles or reviews.

All Scripture quotations are from the Authorized King James Version.

Edited by Laura Nichols, J. R. Faulkner, R. Edward Hampton, and Ann McCollum. Cover and design by Patti Schwartz.

ISBN 0-9752978-0-5

Printed in the United States of America
Spark of Grace Publishers
16810 River Walk
Williamsport, Maryland 21740
(301) 582-0378

Dedicated To:

My sweet mother, Linda G. (Hall) Aikens (in memoriam), who provided me with a foundation.

My darling wife, Holly, who continually provides me with focus.

FOREWORD

The wealth of material to be found within the pages of this book will do far more than meet the requirements for a diploma from an educational institution.

Larry Aikens, Jr. has plumbed the depths of the riches of God's Word to form a biblical foundation upon which to bring to God's servants a wealth of practical knowledge that will benefit all who will take it to heart.

I have read every word on every page and have been blessed, enriched and inspired greatly. Thank you, Brother Aikens.

Dr. J. R. Faulkner
Tennessee Temple University
President Emeritus

PREFACE

Organize or Agonize speaks to every aspect of our lives whether in the home, the workplace, or the church. Herein, Dr. Aikens explores the depths of human nature for both leaders and followers in clarifying the role of each to fortify and reach the ultimate goal of accomplishing great things.

In a very practical way Dr. Aikens explains how to plan to succeed as a leader and how to prudently deal with obstacles which will surface in any organization.

How exciting it would be that young men and women would incorporate the principles in this volume drawn from the Bible into their quest for success.

This volume will meet the need of those who desire to reach their goal with a minimum of stress while helping others maximize their performance.

Dr. R. Edward Hampton
Emmanuel Baptist Temple
Pastor Emeritus

CONTENTS

Introduction 13

Part One: Positional Structure
1. The Importance of Leadership and Followship 19
2. Leadership vs. Followship 23
3. Protecting the Structure 27
4. Positional Structure within the Church 31
5. Positional Structure within the Home 43

Part Two: Planning and Preparation
6. The Importance of Planning and Preparation 57
7. Determining Your Goal 63
8. Envisioning Obstacles 71
9. Organizing Your Thoughts 77
10. The Most Important Plan of All 81

Part Three: Process of Execution
11. Putting Things in Motion 95
12. Developing Your Team 99
13. Becoming a Team Player 105
14. Leading Your Team 115
15. Following Your Leader 123

Part Four: Power of Follow-through
16. Accountability: Know What Is Going On 131
17. Approaching an Obstacle 137
18. Receiving Instruction 145
19. Clearing an Obstacle 157
20. The Future in Focus 167

Notes 175

Bibliography 177

LUKE 16:1-9

1 And he said also unto his disciples, There was a certain rich man, which had a steward; and the same was accused unto him that he had wasted his goods.

2 And he called him, and said unto him, How is it that I hear this of thee? Give an account of thy stewardship; for thou mayest be no longer steward.

3 Then the steward said within himself, What shall I do? For my lord taketh away from me the stewardship: I cannot dig; to beg I am ashamed.

4 I am resolved what to do, that, when I am put out of the stewardship, they may receive me into their houses.

5 So he called every one of his lord's debtors unto him, and said unto the first, How much owest thou unto my lord?

6 And he said, An hundred measures of oil. And he said unto him, Take thy bill, and sit down quickly, and write fifty.

7 Then said he to another, And how much owest thou? And he said, An hundred measures of wheat. And he said unto him, Take thy bill, and write fourscore.

8 And the lord commended the unjust steward, because he had done wisely: *for the children of this world are in their generation wiser than the children of light.*

9 And I say unto you, Make to yourselves friends of the mammon of unrighteousness; that, when ye fail, they may receive you into everlasting habitations.

INTRODUCTION

At last, business was booming. From its humble beginning the operation had grown to have a major presence in the marketplace. Relieved, the owner began to enjoy his success after a lifetime of diligent labor.

Throughout the years the owner had grown to trust one of the employees within his organization. As the demands of the business increased he had promoted this man through the ranks of management, recently naming him Chief Executive Officer. This man had been proven trustworthy and the company was running so smoothly that the owner found himself relying more and more upon his leadership in the day-to-day operation of the business. This gave him freedom to pursue other interests and relieved much of the stress he had been living with. It seemed that finally he had the time to enjoy life coupled with the financial freedom to live his dreams. Everything was going so well, until one day a problem surfaced within the organization.

A group of employees approached the owner and accused their Chief Executive Officer of mismanaging the business. Some claimed the officer was investing the company assets for personal gain. Others charged the officer with inattentiveness to business, resulting in heavy losses. Still others felt the decisions he was making were detrimental to the future of the company. The owner was alarmed by the discontentment they expressed, but the accusations they had made were serious and demanded resolution.

Deeply troubled, the owner tried to sort out the information he had been given. He hesitated to believe anything negative about this officer—this was not the first time that employees had criticized management; however, what they had said was set against a backdrop of recent suspicion he had tried to ignore. He recalled a meeting with his CEO several weeks before where they had discussed an unusual decline in the business. The officer had convinced him that the market was sluggish and brighter days were just ahead. This had alleviated his concern at the time, but now serious doubts crept in again. What was really going on? He determined that one way or the other he would get to the bottom of this—the man must be held responsible for the decline in the business and solid proof would be sought for any excuses he might give.

The owner called in the officer and told him of the recent accusations. The officer, finding himself under close scrutiny, defended his actions, but could not present evidence to support his reasoning. The owner, struggling with the decision of who to believe, ordered a full-scale audit of the company. He informed the officer that if the charges were found to be true, he would have no choice but to terminate his employment.

The officer left the meeting deeply troubled. Perhaps he knew the investigation would be incriminating, or maybe he felt the owner was bent on implicating him in the recent failures of the business. Either way, he could see the handwriting on the wall.

His thoughts immediately focused on the future. He realized his present employer was not going to give him a favorable recommendation. He knew he faced some huge problems that would have to be solved if he was ever to be employed again in the same line of work. He weighed his options carefully. He could easily find an entry-level job, but there would be a great reduction of salary, not to mention the humiliating aspect of manual labor. Besides, he just couldn't let one negative situation ruin what he had been building his entire career. In his mind he vowed to never accept charity—he had worked too long and hard to now admit that he was unable to support himself or make his own way. He just couldn't let the odds overwhelm him; somehow he would overcome this hurdle and move forward in his career.

He devised a clever plan. He would take this bad situation, turn it around, and make it work for his future. The owner's resources and reputation would give him the platform he needed to launch a job search and influence potential employers.

So with the audit in progress, the officer quickly set his plan in motion. Diversifying his opportunities, he called every one of the owner's debtors in. Taking full advantage of the position he still held, he cut each of them a tremendous deal—settling their debts at bargain prices. He had people refinancing and consolidating debt all over town. Untold dollars were lost—not only in principle, but also in interest.

Soon this was discovered and, of course, it brought the whole situation to a head, producing the meeting to end all meetings. The owner declared the officer to be unjust and released him from his service; however, he couldn't help but express his admiration, commending the officer for shrewdness and foresight in providing for his future. The owner realized the officer's stroke of genius had completely outmaneuvered him. He found himself beaten at his own game and with dignity congratulated his opponent.

In Luke 16, verse 8, notice the commentary of Jesus on the story of this unjust steward: "For the children of this world are in their generation wiser than the children of light." Can you imagine Jesus saying that? Literally, Jesus states that people who are unsaved, in promoting the interests of this world are more clever than people who know the truth of salvation, have the Holy Spirit dwelling within them, and are promoting the interests of Christ. Albert Barnes, in his *Notes on the New Testament Explanatory and Practical: Luke and John*, explains it so well it is worth repeating word for word:

> ...*Are wiser.* More prudent, cunning, and anxious about their particular business. They show more skill, study more plans, contrive more ways to provide for themselves, than the children of light do to promote the interests of religion.[1]

This statement made by Jesus ought to captivate our conscience and propagate our imagination as we consider the reality that much more has been done to promote the interests of business than to promote the Lord Jesus Christ.

Everywhere we look today, we see business bulging. Great corporations have skyrocketed over the past century—many with a worldwide presence. The stock market has grown unbelievably. In fact, during a relatively short existence, the United States of America has gone from its humble beginning to a prosperous super-power with a presence felt worldwide.

You need not take painstaking inventory of the church ("children of light") to realize the full weight of Jesus' statement. The church had its foundation in Jesus Christ some two thousand years ago, and yet it seems comparatively little has been accomplished. There have been some bright spots along the way, but we must confess that in our day, more than ever, believers and unbelievers are much more diligent in secular business than believers are in serving the Lord Jesus Christ.

> *The church had its foundation in Jesus Christ some two thousand years ago, and yet it seems comparatively little has been accomplished.*

Now that we have seen Jesus' commentary on the story in verse eight, see His direct application in verse nine: "And I say unto you, Make to yourselves friends of the mammon of unrighteousness." Businesses have a "bottom line" and so much is done to ensure success in meeting those earthly objectives. We also have a "bottom line" of winning precious souls to the Saviour and we should use earthly means to see that this goal is accomplished. Jesus never suggested that we do anything unjust or dishonest, but He did instruct us to use the principles of sound business found in Luke 16 to build His Kingdom.

The motivation for our work is found in the last part of verse nine, "That, when ye fail, they may receive you into everlasting habitations." Literally, when we die, the folks we have won to the Saviour will welcome us into Heaven. Jesus reminds us that one day this life will be over and eternity will begin. Then all these earthly pursuits will vanish, but the lives we have touched with the gospel will live on in Heaven for eternity. To think, the work He has called us to changes the eternal destiny of people! What could be more important than that?

There are four foundational areas of organization in this story Jesus told: positional structure, planning and preparation, process of execution, and power of follow-through. Within these four broad-based areas we will examine valuable principles that provide an infrastructure upon which individual lives, homes, churches, organizations, and the efforts of Christianity in general grow and prosper. They are absolutely essential for organizational strength. If violated, the very foundation will crumble.

PART ONE

Positional Structure

CHAPTER ONE

The Importance of Leadership and Followship

As the story of the unjust steward is just beginning, we are brought face to face with a fundamental principle of organization:

When you are supposed to lead, lead;

When you are supposed to follow, follow.

Society is made up of leaders and followers. To be organizationally strong, there must be an understanding and strong adherence to this principle. At times we all need to be followers and at times we are called upon to be leaders. The key is understanding the role we are to play and performing it to the best of our ability.

So many organizations have been extremely successful because the people understood leadership and followship. Others have failed because they did not adhere to this basic principle. When people cannot determine who is in charge they never accomplish much, because they are

> *There are only three types of people, organizationally speaking. A person is a leader, a follower, or he becomes an obstacle in the way of progress.*

constantly pulling in separate directions. This power struggle results in defeat for everyone in the organization.

There are only three types of people, organizationally speaking. A person is a leader, a follower, or he becomes an obstacle in the way of progress. When a leader refuses to take responsibility to lead in an area where he should be leading, but will not step aside to allow someone else to lead, it results in him becoming an obstacle—in the way of the organization moving forward. The same can be said of a follower. When someone who should be following deludes himself and pursues his own path, or worse yet attempts to place himself in the position of leadership, he becomes a barricade in the path of others who are cooperating and getting things done. Oh, that God would open our eyes that we might understand where we ought to lead and then lead there to the best of our ability. Likewise, we must understand where we ought to follow and then place ourselves there, wholeheartedly under leadership, supporting our leader with all our might.

There are some truths about people who become obstacles:

Obstacles become *Spectacles*;
Spectacles create *Diversions*;
Diversions result in *Ineffectiveness*.

It is not long until an *obstacle* will focus attention on himself and create *diversion*, getting focus off the goal. When the goal is not recognized, everybody within the organization loses.

Let me illustrate the point. While managing the operations of a rental car company, we found this to be an ongoing problem. At each rental location, there were three employees: a location manager, an assistant manager, and a fleet agent. The management primarily focused on sales and providing customer service. The fleet agents were to support their position by maintaining the serviceability and cleanliness of the rental vehicles. Most of the fleet agents' work was outside in the elements and demanded physical labor. The management's duties required them to be inside most of the time and this taxed their mental and relational skills. The problems usually were generated because of this contrast in the work environment and duties of the management versus the fleet agent. Time and again the fleet agents were reminded that their contribution was of equal importance to the success of the team—customer service depended upon providing clean, well-serviced vehicles; but the fleet agents would begin to ignore their job and try to perform the functions of the management. This resulted in lost sales, poor customer service, and disgruntled employees.

I remember one incident in particular. One of our fleet agents heard about an opening for a management position at one of the locations. He decided he would like to be promoted to management, so he sent in a request. Unfortunately, during the several months that he had been with the company, he had not received a satisfactory review from his management concerning his training. They were still working with him, trying to secure acceptable service for the fleet. Of course, his request was denied and he was reminded about the importance of the job that he had been hired to do. From that point on his performance began to go down and he did as little as he could to just get by. He spent more and more time inside the store—getting in the way of customer service and sales–and the vehicles suffered.

One day, one of the cars that he should have been maintaining broke down while on rent to a customer. The customer came back to the location, very dissatisfied and angry. Before the customer could get inside the store, the fleet agent met him outside on the lot. Untrained in handling customer problems, the agent started a heated argument with the customer. During one of the busiest times of the day, a shouting match was taking place in front of the store! Needless to say, we lost a customer and an employee that day, damaging the company and impacting the bottom line. This employee became an obstacle; as an obstacle he made a spectacle; the spectacle created diversion; and the diversion resulted in ineffectiveness.

We all could tell story after story illustrating the truth of this point. One of the most difficult things we will ever do is maintain positional structure, but the organization that majors on this point will be fundamentally well on its way.

CHAPTER TWO

Leadership vs. Followship

First of all, let's define what it takes to be a good follower. The word "follower" could be replaced with the word "imitator," "mimic," or "impersonator." Part of Webster's definition for the root word, "follow," gives this description: "to act in accordance with; to accept the authority of; obey [to follow rules]; to support or advocate the ideas, opinions, etc. of."[2] Simply put, a follower would be one who patterns after another who is leading. Early in this discussion, it should be stated that following is not really following until the leader leads in a direction that the follower does not agree with or is not already going in. There are several points about leaders and followers that ought to be expounded.

Wise leaders will surround themselves with many followers. They reproduce themselves by training, inspiring, and giving their job away—then they take on more. This is the law of multiplication. A person who tries to do everything will be a "jack of all trades, but master of none."

A one-person show will only be as effective as that one person is. Leaders blessed with true followers will be able to reproduce themselves in the lives of many people, thereby increasing their effectiveness for Christ one hundred, one-thousand, or even ten-thousand fold.

Wise leaders will learn all they can from their followers and wise followers will learn all they can from their leaders. Never forget—everyone brings something to the table from which we can learn. I'll never forget a lesson in character I learned from a most unlikely place—a salvage yard. Right before Holly and I married, there were several months of waiting and looking for our first opportunity in the ministry. My dad has a friend who owns an auto salvage business and I approached him about a temporary job. I don't believe I have ever worked harder, gotten dirtier, and made less money than I did during those several months! The manager there told me when I first came to work, "Some folks get a lot of money, we just get a lot of hours!" It wasn't long until I realized he was right. I have never seen anybody before or since who hustled any more than he, but my story is not about him. It's about the lead man out in the yard we'll call "Billy."

Billy had been pulling parts off wrecked cars for years. It was hard to carry on a conversation with Billy because he was uneducated and spoke with a pronounced speech impediment. Billy was probably about forty-five years old, but he looked sixty-five. Because of his job (and mine, too) he always had on filthy clothes, full of grease and dirt. I don't think he shaved but once a week, and for that matter, probably did not take a bath more often than that either. Billy always looked like he had just crawled out from under a car. Who knows, he may have slept out on the lot somewhere; but he was always there early in the morning, ready to work.

At first I tried to steer clear of him and do my work, but I found myself constantly running into problems taking off parts and I would have to seek out Billy. There was no part that Billy could not remove. One day I was trying to take a driver's side glass out of a Ford car that had been seriously wrecked. The door was smashed in, but miraculously the glass had survived the impact. A customer was on his way to buy that particular piece of glass. The boss sent me to take the glass out, warning me to be careful because that was the only glass like it on the property. I climbed inside and all around that vehicle trying to get the glass out. You see, you have to take the interior plastic piece off the door, roll down the window, loosen the bolts that hold the glass in place, and then the glass will slide up and out of the doorframe.

The problem was the door was smashed against the driver's seat where it would not open. I could not figure out how to get the plastic piece off and get the window down. After trying for awhile and getting frustrated, I decided Billy would have to get the torch and cut the door away, salvaging the glass. I went to get Billy. I told him he would need his torch, but he said, "I don't need no torch to get that glass out—come here." I followed Billy back to the car. He immediately crawled into the passenger side, laid down on the seat, and proceeded to give the driver's door several hard kicks with his boot. The door popped open. Out crawled Billy with a big toothless grin across his face. He looked at me and said, "If you keep working hard out here, one day you will be just like me!" He then turned and walked away. My first thought was, "Why would I ever want to be like him?" Later on that day, I reflected on the incident and realized Billy had taught me a valuable lesson. He had taught me determination. In my mind, he holds the place of being the most determined man I have ever been around . . . Billy always got his part!

> *...wise followers will seek to promote their leader and wise leaders will seek to promote their followers, thereby promoting the cause of Christ.*

We can learn something from everybody if we will just open our mind and be receptive to those around us. Isn't that what the Scripture admonishes us to do? "Wherefore, my beloved brethren, let every man be swift to hear, slow to speak, slow to wrath: for the wrath of man worketh not the righteousness of God" (James 1:19-20). There are certain times in life when you are called upon to follow a leader who is less qualified, less visionary, or less educated than you are—and perhaps is doing things "all wrong." It is so easy to grow impatient and critical of others' faults rather than try to learn from them—even if the lessons are about what not to do. At other times you will be called upon to lead people who you do not respect. Always remember that you can learn something from everyone and everyone is important to your sucessful service for Christ.

Another point to stress: wise followers will seek to promote their leader and wise leaders will seek to promote their followers, thereby promoting the cause of Christ. Interestingly enough, every follower of Christ desires their life to make a difference, but so many short-circuit their connection to success by evading one of its basic components: you will be no better than the people with whom you surround yourself. Leaders will go no farther than the strength of the team they build, and the team will be no stronger than the leader they inspire. You can never weaken a link in a chain and expect it to hold up to the demands of the job. A chain is only as good as its weakest link, and I propose to you that poor followship creates poor leadership and poor leadership creates poor followship, resulting in failure to reach our potential for Christ.

Dr. Lee Roberson is well known for saying, "Everything rises and falls on leadership." The flip side of the coin is, "Where would a leader be without good followers?" When I was about to accept my first position in the ministry as a youth and music director, I called Dr. J.R. Faulkner, longtime associate to Dr. Roberson, for his advice. I asked him what it took to be an effective associate. He shared with me several bits of advice that have stuck with me. First of all, he said that he had tried to make himself valuable to Dr. Roberson. He had tried to determine how to be a good follower and then performed that role to the best of his ability. Secondly, he had always tried to promote Dr. Roberson. In using the word "promote" he explained that as an associate he had done all in his power to assist Dr. Roberson in carrying out the vision that God had given him for that ministry. He described it as pushing Dr. Roberson up the ladder ahead of him. Because he had made himself valuable to Dr. Roberson, he knew that if he pushed Dr. Roberson up a rung, he in turn would reach down and pull him up right behind him.

I believe the rewards in Heaven will be great for the many who have seen their role and calling as a follower and have set out to promote their leader with all their might. In like fashion, the leaders who have promoted their followers have found their responsibilities enhanced and the effectiveness of the team strengthened. The bottom line of the whole matter is this: followers and leaders must consider themselves part of a team—each important, each relying on the other, but the leader leading and the followers following their leadership.

CHAPTER THREE

Protecting the Structure

In a perfect world, there would be leaders leading and followers following all the time. There would never be a situation like what is presented in Luke 16 with the unjust steward. There was obviously a problem figuring out who was at the helm and who was at the oar. The unjust steward seemed to be pulling in a direction opposite of the owner, refusing to follow leadership.

This is probably one of the most common problems in all organizations today, if not a basic problem in our whole society. Managers spend most of their time dealing with problems created by violations of this basic principle on both sides of the issue—not only followers who will not follow, but also leaders who will not lead. We have explored the wonders of teamwork when leaders lead and their followers follow, but there have been so many people who destroy themselves and their organizations while ignoring this principle altogether. We must then ask ourselves an obvious question, "Why is there not better cooperation; why is it so hard for people to grasp this simple concept?"

The problem is rooted back in the beginning of time when Lucifer, one of God's angels, exalted himself against God's leadership and was cast out of Heaven. In Satan's ongoing rebellion against God, he tempted Adam and Eve, the first humans God created, to disobey God's commandment. They chose to do so, disregarding God's leadership over their lives; thereby incurring a fallen sinful nature. This sinful nature has been passed on to every one of us according to Romans 5:12, "Wherefore, as by one man sin entered into the world, and death by sin; and so death passed upon all men, for that all have sinned." The problem of maintaining structure within any organization is a heart problem among its people (a sin problem) inherited by the fallen nature. "The heart is deceitful above all things, and desperately wicked: who can know it?" (Jeremiah 17:9). As long as there are people, there will be challenges to solve if positional structure is to be maintained within any organization.

In our text, the rich man protected the structure of his organization. In later chapters we will explore the action he took and examine strategies to handle problems; but notice that when he heard of a problem he went to the source, sought out the truth, and acted upon the result of his findings. One can only imagine how trying the circumstances must have been, but he made a dedicated effort to solve the problem that was hindering the progress of his organization.

Everyone in an organization should be strongly committed to protecting the structure. The problems that arise must be addressed and solved. Often this involves difficult confrontations with resulting decisions that are uncomfortable, but leaders and followers alike should desire and support action when taken to remove obstacles that will ensure the success of the organization. Remember what happens when people become *obstacles*? An *obstacle* soon becomes a *spectacle*; it is not long until a *spectacle* creates *diversion*; and the *diversion* he creates results in *ineffectiveness* for the organization. With this in mind it is easy to see that, when the structure is protected, everyone within the organization benefits.

While at the rental car company, I was promoted quite rapidly. Within four months, I was appointed the vice-president of operations, after having started as a manager-trainee in one of the locations. This caused quite a stir among the employees in the field. They felt passed over for promotion and discontentment was spreading. In my newly found role as leader, I rapidly found myself with no followers. All the employees in operations were becoming huge *obstacles* to forward motion. One day, we almost had a huge *spectacle*—word around the corporate office was that everyone had threatened to walk off the job, leaving the locations with no personnel. Wow, what a *diversion* that would be!

When I heard what was being rumored, I went to the owner and outlined the complications. He called in two of the top location managers who we felt to be ringleaders in the opposition against his decision. He called them into the office one at a time with their district manager and asked them what was going on out in the field. They would not give him straight answers at first, but finally they began to present their case in opposing his recent appointment. He discussed with them some of his reasoning. The first was satisfied and went back to work, pledging to support my appointment. The second manager was still unsatisfied. The owner got up out of his chair behind the executive desk. He asked this person to sit in his chair behind the desk. He then sat in the guest chair across from the manager, looked this person in the eye, and said something like this, "When you can buy me out of that chair, then you can call the shots around here, but as long as I sit in that chair, I'll make the decisions." I never had any more trouble out of that employee. In fact, over a period of time this person became one of my most loyal employees and I promoted that person to be a district manager under my office. This would have never been possible had the structure not been protected.

> *Outside the structure, there is strife;*
>
> *Within the structure, there is life.*

I am convinced the greatest contribution you can make to any organization is to protect the structure. If you are a leader, deal with the obstacles. If you are a follower, support leadership that will clear away obstacles for the progress of the organization.

CHAPTER FOUR

Positional Structure within the Church

I believe there is no subject dearer to Christ's heart than the Church. In fact, Christ loves the Church so much that Ephesians 5:25 says, "He gave Himself for it." Christ sacrificially gave His life on the cross that the Church might be brought into existence. Of course, this verse is speaking to the Church as a whole, encompassing all those who have been redeemed by the precious blood of Jesus Christ. However, we know the local church is a visible assembly of those redeemed, who have associated themselves for the purposes of promoting the gospel and building up the family of God. The simplest expression of the local church is found in Matthew 18:20, "For where two or three are gathered together in my name, there am I in the midst of them."

So many believers have "gathered together in *Jesus* name" with a wonderful desire to build an organization for Christ, but have lost their effectiveness because they did not have the correct positional structure. The Bible says in Ephesians 2:20b-21, "Jesus Christ himself being the chief corner stone; in whom all the building fitly framed together groweth unto an holy temple in the Lord." There could be no other organization on earth where it is more important to understand positional structure than the church, but there is much controversy about who is supposed to lead the church and exactly when he is supposed to lead. Also, it is debated who is supposed to follow and exactly when is he supposed to follow. It seems there is a need for Biblical, straightforward counsel to be given on this subject. For this counsel, we will focus our attention on Joshua, chapter one.

In this passage, Moses has just died and Joshua is being installed as the new leader of Israel. Down through history, God has always chosen a leader to accomplish His goals. From this account we see God's basic design of leadership and followship unfold and we draw three basic applications for the local church, mirrored throughout Scripture, and emphasized in the New Testament.

> *So many believers have "gathered together in Jesus name"...but have lost their effectiveness because they did not have the correct positional structure.*

Commissioning the Leader

Joshua 1:1-9

1 Now after the death of Moses the servant of the LORD it came to pass, that the LORD spake unto Joshua the son of Nun, Moses' minister, saying,

2 Moses my servant is dead; now therefore arise, go over this Jordan, thou, and all this people, unto the land which I do give to them, even to the children of Israel.

3 Every place that the sole of your foot shall tread upon, that have I given unto you, as I said unto Moses.

4 From the wilderness and this Lebanon even unto the great river, the river Euphrates, all the land of the Hittites, and unto the great sea toward the going down of the sun, shall be your coast.

5 There shall not any man be able to stand before thee all the days of thy life: as I was with Moses, so I will be with thee: I will not fail thee, nor forsake thee.

6 Be strong and of a good courage: for unto this people shalt thou divide for an inheritance the land, which I sware unto their fathers to give them.

7 Only be thou strong and very courageous, that thou mayest observe to do according to all the law, which Moses my servant commanded thee: turn not from it to the right hand or to the left, that thou mayest prosper whithersoever thou goest.

8 This book of the law shall not depart out of thy mouth; but thou shalt meditate therein day and night, that thou mayest observe to do according to all that is written therein: for then thou shalt make thy way prosperous, and then thou shalt have good success.

9 Have not I commanded thee? Be strong and of a good courage; be not afraid, neither be thou dismayed: for the LORD thy God is with thee whithersoever thou goest.

In the first several verses above, notice how Joshua is commissioned to lead God's people after the death of Moses, "[. . .] the LORD spake unto Joshua [. . .] arise, go over this Jordan, thou, and all this people, unto the land which I do give to them, even to the children of Israel" (vs. 1-2). As relating to positional structure within the church it is foundational to understand that any authority to lead in the church must have its source in Jesus Christ since He is the Founder and Head of the Church. There has never been a man with enough experience, intelligence, education, or strength to ever be qualified within himself to lead the flock of God. Clearly, the local church pastor is chosen and equipped by God Himself. The Apostle Paul gave this testimony concerning his divine calling to the ministry, "And I thank Christ Jesus our Lord, who hath enabled me, for that he counted me faithful, putting me into the ministry" (I Timothy 1:12). Further, God places a pastor in a particular church. God says in Jeremiah 3:15, "And I will give you pastors according to mine heart, which shall feed you with knowledge and understanding."

Jesus Christ is the head of the Church and represents Himself with a human instrument, the pastor, through whom He leads and instructs each local assembly. Notice that God gave clear instructions to Joshua and then affirmed his leadership in verse five, "There shall not any man be able to stand before thee all the days of thy life: as I was with Moses, so I will be with thee: I will not fail thee, nor forsake thee." Several times in Scripture God issues a strong warning, "Touch not mine anointed, and do my prophets no harm" (Psalms 105:15, I Chronicles 16:22). Plainly, God gives His servants authority to lead in their area of responsibility with the expectation that His people will follow their leadership.

God has set a high performance standard for leadership. Just as Joshua was given an overwhelming task, the pastor of a local church is responsible to lead the believers of the local assembly in the task of taking the gospel to "the uttermost part of the earth," beginning with "Jerusalem" first (Acts 1:8). No wonder God told Joshua, "Be strong and of a good courage [. . .] be thou strong and very courageous [. . .]" (Joshua 1:6-7a). Not only did Joshua need encouragement to fulfill the great tasks that were ahead, he would also need accountability. God admonished His new leader to conduct the affairs of the nation according to all the principles that He had given Moses. Further, God gave Joshua this personal mandate, "This book of the law shall not depart out of thy mouth; but thou shalt meditate therein day and night, that thou mayest observe to do according to all that is written therein." Likewise, a pastor has been made accountable to God for how he leads the local church as well as how he lives his personal life.

God's closing comments to Joshua should resound in the ears of pastors who represent His authority in the Church, "Have not I commanded thee? Be strong and of a good courage; be not afraid, neither be thou dismayed: for the LORD thy God is with thee whithersoever thou goest" (Joshua 1:9). He is ever present, keeping accurate records of how His leaders are carrying out His work.

When you read Scripture, you find that although God is merciful, He is just. God can and will handle His management problems. Think of God's leader, Moses. He was not allowed to see the Promised Land because of his disobedience to the Lord (see Deuteronomy 34:1-8). The Apostle Paul seemed to understand he was accountable to God, "I keep under my body, and bring it unto subjection: lest that by any means, when I have preached to others, I myself should be a castaway" (I Corinthians 9:27). He will deal with the pastors who become obstacles. We must trust in His divine knowledge of the situation. He knows whether the problem is with the leader or the follower and will mete out justice according to His sovereign will.

I have been in hundreds of churches across America. Having been in forty-two states, traveling from local church to local church, I have observed that this truth is often ignored. People, professing to do the work of the Lord, have stood against the man of God time and time again. I do not pretend to say that every pastor has always been correct in what he has done. Sometimes it seemed that his followers had a valid complaint. On the other hand, many times the followers have not been surrendered to God's will. At any rate, they have gotten in the way of God's dealing with the situation and have brought much hurt and shame to themselves personally and to the work of the Lord.

I remember one case in particular. I preached at a church located in a large, metropolitan area. The evening before I preached, one of the deacons gave me a tour of the buildings. We walked into a large auditorium, which seated well over eight hundred people. After admiring its beauty, we ascended a long flight of stairs up to the baptismal pool. Instead of steps, there were two long walkways, like wheel-chair ramps, going into the baptistry. There was no water in the pool, so I walked down the ramp admiring the magnificent view of the auditorium. I could tell the mood of the deacon was somber as we descended back to the auditorium. We stopped in front of the pulpit and the deacon told me a thought-provoking story.

He said the church had really experienced the blessings of God under a pastor who had left there about twenty-five years before. Under that pastor's leadership the church had grown from about two hundred to over eight hundred! Wistfully, he said he could remember a time when the baptistry was being used every Sunday. Now, he continued, the church held barely two hundred on a good Sunday morning, the evening service was less than half that, and the baptistry certainly was not in regular use. With no coercion on my part, he went on to say something that impressed upon me his understanding of this point: "We lost the blessings of God because of the way we handled that pastor. The church has never been the same since."

He went on to explain, "The pastor's wife was having some problems. We [board of deacons] found out about them and quickly had a meeting with the pastor. We asked him to resign, feeling the problems would be a stumbling block to the ministry. Confusion in the church resulted and we lost hundreds of people overnight. Things went steadily downhill and we have never seen the moving of God again." He concluded with all the seriousness only twenty-five years of regret could muster, "I wish we would have let God handle the situation—he was God's man and God could have removed him if that was His will."

Carrying Out God's Plan

Joshua 1:10-15

10 Then Joshua commanded the officers of the people, saying,

11 Pass through the host, and command the people, saying, Prepare you victuals; for within three days ye shall pass over this Jordan, to go in to possess the land, which the LORD your God giveth you to possess it.

12 And to the Reubenites, and to the Gadites, and to half the tribe of Manasseh, spake Joshua, saying,

13 Remember the word which Moses the servant of the LORD commanded you, saying, The LORD your God hath given you rest, and hath given you this land.

14 Your wives, your little ones, and your cattle, shall remain in the land which Moses gave you on this side Jordan; but ye shall pass before your brethren armed, all the mighty men of valour, and help them;

15 Until the LORD have given your brethren rest, as he hath given you, and they also have possessed the land which the LORD your God giveth them: then ye shall return unto the land of your possession, and enjoy it, which Moses the LORD's servant gave you on this side Jordan toward the sunrising.

Before we can fully understand the practicality of leadership transferring into followship in the church, we must have more insight into the responsibilities of the pastor. The Scripture gives us a two-sided picture of the position, using three titles to describe the function of the office.

One side of the picture expresses the administrative office with the titles "elder" and "bishop." The flip side brings to surface the ministerial gift, using the title "pastor." A general misconception of Scriptural truth has been the root of confusion in many churches.

First of all, let's examine the administrative office starting with the title "elder." I Timothy 5:17 says, "Let the elders that rule well be counted worthy of double honour, especially they who labour in the word and doctrine." The title of "elder" is not expressive of age, but denotes one who has been brought to a place of leadership in the local church by the selection and calling of God and has been equipped by the power of the Holy Spirit working in and through his life. This book in the Bible was written to a young pastor, Timothy, so this title could not be demonstrative of physical age.

> *The Scripture gives us a two-sided picture of the position, using three titles to describe the function of the office.*

Some interpret this title to be a position on a board of elders in the local church, pointing to the plurality of the word when mentioned in Scripture. This school of thought puts laymen over the administration of the church. This elder board is positionally considered equal to or over the pastor, creating a plurality of leadership. There are three distinct problems with this interpretation of Scripture. First of all, it is inconsistent with God's method throughout Scripture for central leadership of His people. Secondly, when Scripture uses the plural word, "elders," the reference is to an area like Ephesus that contained multiple churches. God's intention is to have one elder for each church and the plural form, "elders," encompasses all of the elders in an area serving individual churches. Thirdly, this creates an unbiblical hierarchy that comes between God's direct leading of His man and causes the leader to report to the followers. This form of positional structure is impractical, awkward, and most of all unscriptural.

The title of "elder" speaks of the pastor's positional authority in the local church; whereas, the title of "bishop" denotes his practical responsibility. Administratively the pastor has not only the authority to lead the spiritual matters of the church, but he has a practical responsibility to manage the physical affairs as well.

The title of "bishop" is translated "overseer" in Acts 20:28, "Take heed therefore unto yourselves, and to all the flock, over the which the Holy Ghost hath made you *overseers*, to feed the church of God, which he hath purchased with his own blood." In I Timothy 3, we are given the Scriptural qualifications for the office of bishop and deacon. The qualifications are almost identical, with one clear exception. The question posed in verse five, "(For if a man know not how to rule his own house, how shall he take care of the church of God?)" refers to the office of a bishop. Although the office of a deacon requires a man to rule his children and home well, there is no mention of him having responsibility to oversee the church.

Now, as we turn the picture over, the ministry gift surfaces with the title "pastor." Surprisingly enough, the word "pastor" in its singular or plural form is only mentioned nine times in the entire Bible—eight times in Jeremiah, and only once more in Ephesians 4:11. "And he gave some, apostles; and some, prophets; and some, evangelists; and some *pastors* and teachers." The title of "pastor" speaks of a spiritual gift or enablement of the Holy Spirit that allows the man of God to care for the flock. This provided gift empowers the pastor to preach, teach, counsel, comfort, understand, love, bear burdens, and relate in other care-giving functions to the people of God.

> *One of the greatest hindrances to establishing positional structure in the church is unwillingness on the part of church members to allow their God-given leader to function in both a ministry office as well as an administrative office.*

One of the greatest hindrances to establishing positional structure in the church is unwillingness on the part of church members to allow their God-given leader to function in both a ministry office *as well as* an administrative office. There are also pastors who have failed to recognize the full scope of their responsibility and have focused only on their pastoral duties, ignoring their administrative role altogether. Truly a church is well on its way structurally when they allow God's commissioned man to assume leadership over the entire function of the local church.

We have established the pastor's authority and position. Does that mean that he is the only one important to the church? Does he initiate everything? Does he run every detail? Absolutely not! How then does a Godly pastor lead? To answer that question we must go to the guidebook, the Bible. In I Peter 5:1-3, we have a wonderful picture, "The elders which are among you I exhort, who am also an elder, and a witness of the sufferings of Christ, and also a partaker of the glory that shall be revealed: Feed the flock of God which is among you, taking the oversight thereof, not by constraint, but willingly; not for filthy lucre, but of a ready mind; neither as being lords over God's heritage, but being ensamples to the flock."

The pastor equips the saved for ministry by feeding the flock. The Scripture teaches that every saved person is to be promoting the Kingdom of Christ. Ephesians 4:11-12 says, "And he gave [. . .] pastors and teachers; For the perfecting of the saints, for the work of the ministry, for the edifying of the body of Christ." His job is to rally the saved, build a team, and train the team to effectively build up the body of Christ. To do this he must raise up leadership under himself who will be able to take responsibility in specific areas. He will seek out and value the counsel of these followers who are most closely working with him in areas of leadership. He then must constantly teach, motivate, and free believers to serve the Lord in ministry. That is why the preaching and teaching ministry of the pastor is so important. According to II Timothy 3:16, "All Scripture is given by inspiration of God, and is profitable for doctrine, for reproof, for correction, for instruction in righteousness." No wonder the pastor is commanded: "Preach the word; be instant in season, out of season; reprove, rebuke, exhort with all longsuffering and doctrine" (II Timothy 4:2).

The pastor also leads by shepherding the flock. This involves guarding against false teaching and doctrine, ministering to their needs with a servant's heart, and setting a good example.

I Peter 5:3 ends on a personal note by reminding us that a pastor is not a lord over the people of God. He should lead the church corporately, but allow the Holy Spirit to work in individual hearts. He should recognize that his leadership among individuals is through his responsibility of sharing and living forth the truth, but the people of his flock are responsible to God for the decisions they make regarding how that truth will relate to their lives. II Timothy 2:24-26 sheds more light on the attitude of the pastor regarding his spiritual leadership: "And the servant of the Lord must not strive; but be gentle unto all men, apt to teach, patient, in meekness instructing those that oppose themselves; if God peradventure will give them repentance to the acknowledging of the truth; and that they may recover themselves out of the snare of the devil, who are taken captive by him at his will."

In summary, the pastor is to carry out God's plan through a team effort of the people of God. Remember the direct leadership of Joshua? "Then Joshua commanded the officers of the people [. . .]" (vs. 10). What a wonderful day in the life of a local church when people begin to follow their pastor, the leader God has placed over them! Let's consider an analogy from the world of sports. The pastor to the church is what the head coach is to a professional football team. A head coach is completely ineffective without a structure beneath him of both leaders and followers, and obviously would not be the head coach if the owner had not placed him in that position. The owner and the entire team look to this leader for harmonious functioning that will result in games being won. Can you imagine a football team without a head coach? What if there was a gut-wrenching, game-breaking decision late in the fourth quarter?

> *...the pastor is to carry out God's plan through a team effort of the people of God.*

. . . Suppose it is fourth down with four yards to go. The home team is down by six, but is in scoring position on the twenty-yard line. The special teams coach is shouting for the sure-fire field goal and a last-ditch effort at an onside kick, while the offensive line coach argues for the running play, insisting they could make first down. The defensive coordinator votes with the special teams coach, believing his defense will force a big turnover, while the offensive coordinator is determined to give his star running back a chance to shine. Tension is running high . . . any play could make or break the game . . . who would make the call?

Cooperation of God's People

Joshua 1:16-18

16 And they answered Joshua, saying, All that thou commandest us we will do, and whithersoever thou sendest us, we will go.

17 According as we hearkened unto Moses in all things, so will we hearken unto thee: only the LORD thy God be with thee, as he was with Moses.

18 Whosoever he be that doth rebel against thy commandment, and will not hearken unto thy words in all that thou commandest him, he shall be put to death: only be strong and of a good courage.

Look at the response of the Children of Israel to Joshua's leadership. What a classic case of cooperation! As humorous as a football team would be without a head coach, it would even be more ridiculous for there to be a head coach and no football team. What if all the players and other coaches decided to quit because they did not get to be the head coach?

You sure wouldn't win many games. Likewise, if the people of God are to accomplish God's will, there must be a cooperative team effort.

The people of God willingly followed Joshua's leadership as unto the Lord. What a great lesson for the local church. If we could remove the personality and focus on Christ, not only would there be greater consistency in our service, but also a greater unity in our efforts. Apostle Paul admonished the Corinthians, "Be ye followers of me, even as I also am of Christ" (I Corinthians 11:1).

Also, if we look past the man, understanding he is a representative of the Lord, we will be able to honor the position regardless of the man. Notice how they transferred their loyalty from Moses to Joshua—instantly pledging their support. What clear instruction is found for the local church in Hebrews 13:17, "Obey them that have the rule over you, and submit yourselves: for they watch for your souls, as they that must give account, that they may do it with joy, and not with grief: for that is unprofitable for you."

Not only would the children of Israel pray for Joshua, but they would also protect the structure under his leadership. Now, please, before we go off the deep end, a major difference between the children of Israel's day and our day must be pointed out. Then, they operated under Law that protected the structure with a sentence of death to any who might oppose God's leadership. Thankfully, today we live under grace and that requirement has been lifted by the New Testament covenant of the blood of Christ. However, the New Testament does still require the church to protect the structure of leadership—only the method has changed. Romans 16:17-18 is very clear, "Now I beseech you, brethren, mark them which cause divisions and offences contrary to the doctrine which ye have learned; and avoid them. For they that are such serve not our Lord Jesus Christ, but their own belly; and by good words and fair speeches deceive the hearts of the simple."

May we put these principles of leadership and followship to work in our local churches all across this land so that positional structure might be protected and promoted for the glory and honor of our Lord Jesus Christ and the advancement of His Church.

CHAPTER FIVE

Positional Structure within the Home

God has instituted four basic building blocks of society: individual life, the home, the local church, and government. Each of these blocks are interrelated and dependent on the other; however, the foundational block is the home. Never before has the foundation been under heavier attack—threatening the family unit to be a lesson in history unless serious measures are taken to repair the structure. No wonder our society has hit a toboggan slide downhill! How the home needs strengthening!

Opening the Bible to Colossians 3:17-21, we find clear instruction about positional structure for the home from the Master Designer himself:

> **17** And whatsoever ye do in word or deed, do all in the name of the Lord Jesus, giving thanks to God and the Father by him.

18 Wives, submit yourselves unto your own husbands, as it is fit in the Lord.

19 Husbands, love your wives, and be not bitter against them.

20 Children, obey your parents in all things: for this is well pleasing unto the Lord.

21 Fathers, provoke not your children to anger, lest they be discouraged.

Simply put, the husband has been made responsible to lead the family in love. The wife is to allow her husband to lead, placing herself under his protection and authority. The children are then to be in obedience to mom and dad who have the responsibility to discipline them with wisdom and understanding.

It may seem simple on paper, but we know that pulling this off in actual life is quite another story. The Holy Spirit understands the struggle we have relating to members of our family, and on more than one occasion gives us the key for developing harmony within the context of the family: "Submitting yourselves one to another in the fear of God" (Ephesians 5:21). Notice the verses directly following this principle:

22 Wives, submit yourselves unto your own husbands, as unto the Lord.

23 For the husband is the head of the wife, even as Christ is the head of the church: and he is the saviour of the body.

24 Therefore as the church is subject unto Christ, so let the wives be to their own husbands in every thing.

25 Husbands, love your wives, even as Christ also loved the church, and gave himself for it;

26 That he might sanctify and cleanse it with the washing of water by the word,

27 That he might present it to himself a glorious church, not having spot, or wrinkle, or any such thing; but that it should be holy and without blemish.

28 So ought men to love their wives as their own bodies. He that loveth his wife loveth himself.

29 For no man ever yet hated his own flesh; but nourisheth and cherisheth it, even as the Lord the church.

Specific instructions for husbands and wives are not changed, but the context is expounded upon. A mutual submission is called for, reflecting the inner working of the grace of God in our hearts. This principle is repeated again in I Peter 3, only more detail is given. Interestingly enough, Ephesians mentions mutual submission before giving specific instruction regarding the structure of the family, while I Peter mentions it afterward. Regardless of location, it is apparent this truth is essential to building strong families. Listen to the counsel of I Peter 3:

> 1a Likewise, ye wives, be in subjection to your own husbands [. . .].
>
> 7 Likewise, ye husbands, dwell with them according to knowledge, giving honour unto the wife, as unto the weaker vessel, and as being heirs together of the grace of life; that your prayers be not hindered.
>
> 8 Finally, be ye all of one mind, having compassion one of another, love as brethren, be pitiful, be courteous:
>
> 9 Not rendering evil for evil, or railing for railing: but contrariwise blessing; knowing that ye are thereunto called, that ye should inherit a blessing.
>
> 10 For he that will love life, and see good days, let him refrain his tongue from evil, and his lips that they speak no guile:
>
> 11 Let him eschew evil, and do good; let him seek peace, and ensue it.
>
> 12 For the eyes of the Lord are over the righteous, and his ears are open unto their prayers: but the face of the Lord is against them that do evil.

There are seven ingredients in this passage from I Peter that give practical insight into cooperation, or mutual submission, that is absolutely necessary for a family to function harmoniously.

Develop the Same Goals

As we fragment this passage, breaking down the truths one by one, we find the first ingredient, "Be ye all of one mind" (I Peter 3:8). In order for the family to function there must be a singleness of purpose—the same goals must be developed.

So many homes are literally pulled apart at the seams by the husband striving to achieve his goals, the wife striving to achieve her goals, and the children somewhere in the midst, struggling to find identity—pursuing goals instilled in them by their peers. Amos 3:3 asks an obvious question, "Can two walk together, except they be agreed?" A family must have a central focus and work together for its accomplishment. This focus becomes a fiber bonding the family unit together, making it strong.

In order to develop this oneness of mind there must be an understanding of leadership and followship in the home. Unfortunately, everyone in the family will not agree on every point. When there is a conflict of interest or direction, someone has to shoulder responsibility to make a decision and the others have to support their authority to do so. There is no family that can function with two people at the helm—someone will take the helm and steer the ship. That someone needs to be the Godly husband seeking the will of God for his family and unifying them to function in that direction.

A classic illustration of this truth is found in the family of Joshua. As mentioned in the previous chapter about the church, Joshua had been commissioned by the Lord to lead the children of Israel into the promised land. He makes a tremendous statement about the functioning of his family, "As for me and my house, we will serve the Lord." There is no doubt that Joshua's family had developed the same goals—they were of one mind!

It is critical that this principle be applied to children. Proverbs imparts understanding, "The rod and reproof give wisdom: but a child left to himself bringeth his mother to shame. Correct thy son, and he shall give thee rest; yea, he shall give delight unto thy soul" (Proverbs 29:15&17). Children need consistent parental guidance to develop the right goals. There are serious consequences for neglecting to train children to obey their parents. If children are not taught to respect authority at home, they may never understand how to contribute effectively to a team effort as an adult.

Have Sympathetic Understanding

The next ingredient admonishes us, "Having compassion one of another" (I Peter 3:8). To have compassion is to trade places with someone in your mind and try to understand the challenges that person lives with every day—seeing things from his or her point of view. Let's face it, we all fall short in many areas. Not one of us scores a perfect ten in every area all the time. A family member should never be in a position of having to earn the favor of another. There should be unconditional, sympathetic understanding.

Specifically in the marriage relationship, it helps tremendously to accept your spouse as a partner by grace and not by merit. This allows each person the freedom to be themself. Instead of trying to "pour them into your mold," there is an effort to understand that differences exist. This point alone relieves volumes of resentment created when there are unfulfilled expectations. Accept, right up front, that your spouse will disappoint you at times. This admonishment to understanding encourages you to forgive ahead of time and alleviate the pressure of your spouse to perform to a standard that he or she cannot uphold.

Brotherly Love Must Reign Supreme

Reading on we find the ingredient of, "Love as brethren" (I Peter 3:8). This is a special undeniable love. It is interesting that the type of love we should have in a marriage is compared to brotherly love. This suggests an irrevocable, loyal bond, viewing your spouse as blood kin! Naturally, there is a blood-bond between parents and children, but for some reason it is growing popular today to view the marital relationship as an agreement of representatives from two separate families—almost as if a peace treaty is being signed between two sovereign republics. There is general distrust and suspicion many times on both sides. A marriage will never blossom without mutual trust and loyalty on both sides. The love called for in this ingredient sets aside all others and puts its highest value upon the relationship between husband and wife.

This concept is closely aligned to the earliest statement ever made about the marriage relationship found in Genesis 2:24, "Therefore shall a man leave his father and his mother, and shall cleave unto his wife: and they shall be one flesh." It is the idea of creating a new family with a definite lifelong commitment to one another—to the point of considering two individual lives to be fused into one. Genesis 2:25 goes on to say, "And they [Adam and Eve] were both naked, and were not ashamed." In the context of brotherly love a relationship flourishes. The transparency and commitment bring about a deep sense of belonging that nurtures heartfelt expression.

At a wedding, you have probably seen the unity candle ceremony that symbolizes this truth. The two outer candles are lit by the bride and groom's parents early in the ceremony. Later, the bride and groom each take a lit candle, light the center candle together, and then blow out the outer candles. This signifies several things. First of all, their loyalty is changed as they leave father and mother to form a new home. Secondly, they formally turn their back on the single lives they led and unite as one in marriage.

Relate in Humility

Fourthly we are admonished to, "Be pitiful" (I Peter 3:8). The Greek word, "eusplagchnos" (yoo'-splangkh-nos), translated "pitiful" in this text is the same word translated "tenderhearted" in Ephesians 4:32: "And be ye kind one to another, *tenderhearted*, forgiving one another, even as God for Christ's sake hath forgiven you." "Eusplagchnos" is from the root words "eu," meaning well, and "splagchnon," figuratively meaning to have tender mercy or sympathy deep within one's being.[3] Hence, this command, "Be pitiful," carries the idea of being compassionate or sympathetic enough to realize that just as you have not "arrived," others have not "arrived" either.

> *There is such freedom when you love your spouse for who he or she is and allow God to bring about change in his or her life.*

Concerning a marriage, Dr. James Dobson expresses this point well: "The key to a healthy marriage is to keep your eyes wide open before you wed—and half-closed thereafter."[4] It is a great day in a marriage when a husband realizes that he is not responsible for the actions of his wife and equally important when a wife relinquishes the responsibility of straightening out her husband. It is stifling in a marriage when a husband plays *dad* or *schoolmaster* in relating to his wife. Just as damaging, it is wrong when a wife *polices* the actions of her husband or takes the convicting role of the Holy Spirit. There is such freedom when you love your spouse for who he or she is and allow God to bring about change in his or her life.

In relating to children, remember the instruction in Colossians? "Fathers, provoke not your children to anger, lest they be discouraged." Although God has placed parents in an authoritative role over the children, this is not to be a self-centered, hard-hearted, unflinching, or detached reign of terror. A parent should selflessly train their children with a goal of helping them to reach their full potential. Loving discipline should be administered within the bounds of sympathetic understanding—meeting children on their level and helping them to work through the normal challenges of life. It helps for parents to identify with their children—not accepting or embracing wrongdoing, but remembering they went through similar learning experiences as a child. In other words, as a parent you must correct your children and enforce the boundaries set for their protection; however, any discipline should be administered in a spirit of humility with a definite goal of bringing the child in line with Biblical principles.

Always Maintain Politeness

The next ingredient goes a long way toward strengthening the home base: "Be courteous" (1 Peter 3:8). Sadly, the ones we love the most see us at our worst much of the time. It is easy to become so relaxed around family members and forget or think it unnecessary to be polite. You know this is true: we maintain our best behavior at work or at church, but excuse ourselves at home—thinking it doesn't matter with a thought like, "my spouse, or the children will understand. . ." The Scripture presents a case in opposition to this thought process. Politeness should never be sacrificed as non-essential.

Do you remember the things you did to win the love of your spouse? Doing the very same things that caused you to fall in love will keep you in love. A man should compliment his wife. A woman should build up her husband. Do you remember when you were dating? You could not say enough positive, affirming things about each other. Husband, your wife still likes to hear that she is charming and beautiful. She still wants to know that you like her hair-style. She still needs to hear that she is dressed attractively. Wife, in like respect your husband desires your admiration and respect. He needs to hear that you have confidence in his abilities and that you respect his leadership.

Perhaps, you are thinking that you would do these things if your spouse was *this* or that. Think of it this way: treat your spouse as if he or she is perfect and you will be amazed at how your spouse will strive to prove that you are right. People who love and respect you will "break their neck" to try and give you what they think you expect and need to be fulfilled and happy.

Wife, next time there is a decision to be made where you disagree with his opinion, tell your husband that you trust his judgment and know that he will do what is best for the family. See if he doesn't think twice before making the decision. Husband, start noticing the way your wife dresses or styles her hair and see if she doesn't improve. It is an undeniable fact of life that people want to please the ones they love—so, make this work for you in your marriage.

Along these lines, be careful of degrading jokes. Don't accent the negative qualities of your spouse or children. He may laugh good-naturedly, but inside he may feel slighted and less valuable to the one from whom he needs the most affirmation. Be careful of drawing attention to things that cannot be readily changed. You may have heard of the newlyweds. On their honeymoon, the groom took his bride by the hand and said, "Now that we are married, dear, I hope you won't mind if I mention a few little defects that I've noticed about you." "Not at all," the bride replied with a deceptive sweetness. "It was those little defects that kept me from getting a better husband."[5] Give your family the dignity and respect you would afford a perfect stranger and you will be well on your way to maintaining goodwill and positive feelings among the family.

Another part of being courteous is maintaining a schedule. Although we have made the case for giving a spouse freedom to be themselves and admonished marital partners to relate in humility—relinquishing control of one another to God, there is still something to be said for maintaining accountability within the home. There are several reasons this is so important.

First of all, if everything is aboveboard and there is nothing to hide, then why give Satan an opportunity to create doubt and suspicion in the mind of your spouse. I Timothy 5:14 encourages us to be sensitive to this reality, "[. . .] give none occasion to the adversary to speak reproachfully." A humorous story illustrates this point. When Adam stayed out very late for a few nights, Eve became upset. "You're running around with other women," she charged. "You're being unreasonable," Adam responded, "You're the only woman on earth." The quarrel continued until Adam fell asleep, only to be awakened by someone poking him in the chest. It was Eve. "What do you think you are doing?" Adam demanded. "Counting your ribs," said Eve.[6]

Secondly, it is impolite to be late for an appointment. You say, "Sure I know that, but this is *just* family." Wait a minute—"just family?" If your wife has set an appointment with you to serve dinner at five o'clock and you show up at five-thirty, do you realize that you may have told her with your actions that you don't care about her hard work in the kitchen and further she is not even important enough for you to be on time for an appointment? Maybe you have never seen it that way, but perhaps that is how she sees it. No wonder you get the third degree! Further, wife, if you have agreed to be home from the grocery to relieve your husband of his baby-sitting duties by one-o'clock so he can make his Saturday tee time and you saunter in at one-thirty, what conclusion is he to draw from your actions? Sure, things do come up and no one is on time all the time, but it should be the exception and not the rule. When it is the exception, a spouse will readily understand.

In all of your striving to be polite, don't forget the "sweet-nothings." Please, thank-you, good table manners, good-morning, good-night, men hanging up their clothes and helping around the house, women respecting their husband's "stuff" and refilling his drink, taking an interest in each other's hobbies, children showing respect to their parents, etc. The list could go on and on. Small things that seem so insignificant, but cumulatively go a long way toward creating an environment of mutual respect and concern for one another in the home.

Be Ready to Forgive and Forget

Every member of the family has so many shortcomings and will make his or her fair share of mistakes, so we must put this ingredient to work, "Not rendering evil for evil, or railing for railing: but contrariwise blessing; knowing that ye are thereunto called, that ye should inherit a blessing" (I Peter 3:9). Turning to Romans 12:19-21, we find similar counsel:

> **19** Dearly beloved, avenge not yourselves, but rather give place unto wrath: for it is written, Vengeance is mine; I will repay, saith the Lord.
>
> **20** Therefore if thine enemy hunger, feed him; if he thirst, give him drink: for in so doing thou shalt heap coals of fire on his head.
>
> **21** Be not overcome of evil, but overcome evil with good.

If you truly are willing to forgive and forget, then naturally you will not seek revenge. Just because someone has done you wrong, this does not give you the right to do that person wrong. You always have a choice—make the right choice and maintain the right response.

Along these same lines, the next verse of the text speaks of guarding against wrong reactions, "For he that will love life, and see good days, let him refrain his tongue from evil, and his lips that they speak no guile" (I Peter 3:10). Expect your family to have a bad day every once in awhile—don't make it worse by responding to their bad spirit. Be mature enough to chart your course!

Think of it this way. If you respond to their wrong actions with equally wrong actions, then they have controlled you—at least for the moment. Let me illustrate. Growing up, I had four sisters. Because of this, I consider myself to be somewhat of an expert at aggravating sisters—I had a lot of practice. Fewer things gave me greater delight than picking on my sisters—I loved to hear them squeal. The more they would squeal, the more I would pester. I got such a reputation around the house that my dad bestowed upon me a much deserved nickname, "Bugs." I never analyzed my reason for aggravating the girls—maybe it was that for a moment, I could control them. When they were reacting to my aggravation, I was calling the shots. Of course, the price of this temporary power was high when mom collected the dues! I was outnumbered to start with, but when mom stepped in, there was not much hope of things ever going my way.

There is a right way and a wrong way to handle problems. Certainly reacting to a situation only makes things worse. We should be pro-active in seeking solutions in the context of forgiveness. Once forgiven, there should be a willingness to put it in the past and get on with life. Just a word of caution about forgiveness. Many times forgiveness is not a one-time event. Remember the Lord's Prayer? "And forgive us our debts, as we forgive our debtors" (Matthew 6:12). "As we forgive" suggests an ongoing process—forgiving each time the problem surfaces again in memory or being willing to forgive again and again for multiple offenses.

Be a Peacemaker

The final ingredient, if applied, balances this recipe for harmony in the home. "Let him eschew evil, and do good; let him seek peace, and ensue it" (I Peter 3:11). The word ensue means to follow after, to pursue. Be a part of the solution for peace in the family.

You may have heard about the couple celebrating their 50th wedding anniversary. When the festivities were over, the woman turned to her husband and said, "We've been miserable for 50 years. We've fought every day. We've disagreed on nearly everything, and I am convinced that we can't keep going like this. I have made a commitment to pray that God will help us solve this problem. I'm praying that He will take one of us home. And when He answers my prayer, I'm going to live with my sister in Grand Rapids."[7]

In Conclusion

As you consider these seven truths, perhaps you realize the organization of your home is in need of adjustment. Where do you start? I Peter 3:12 puts everything into perspective, "For the eyes of the Lord are over the righteous, and his ears are open unto their prayers: but the face of the Lord is against them that do evil."

First of all; confess to God *your* shortcomings. On a daily basis, surrender yourself for His help with the areas in which you struggle. Isn't it wonderful that we have a God who hears our prayer? He is willing to help you become the family member He would have you to be, if you will just ask and surrender your will to His.

Secondly, ask the forgiveness of your family and start to put these ingredients to work. Renewing the structure in your home can start with one person—*you!* Over time, you will be amazed at the godly influence your testimony has on other members of your family. Why not start today?

> *Renewing the structure in your home can start with one person—you!*

PART TWO

Planning and Preparation

CHAPTER SIX

The Importance of Planning and Preparation

One does not read the Bible very long until it is plainly seen that God is a God of order and design. He went to great lengths to instruct us of His plan, using sixty-six books to specify His design for mankind. It is incredible the attention that God gives to detail. Pulling an example out of Numbers 4:29-32, we see the amazing mind of God at work:

> **29** As for the sons of Merari, thou shalt number them after their families, by the house of their fathers;
>
> **30** From thirty years old and upward even unto fifty years old shalt thou number them, every one that enter-eth into the service, to do the work of the tabernacle of the congregation.

31 And this is the charge of their burden, according to all their service in the tabernacle of the congregation; the boards of the tabernacle, and the bars thereof, and the pillars thereof, and sockets thereof,

32 And the pillars of the court round about, and their sockets, and their pins, and their cords, with all their instruments, and with all their service: and by name ye shall reckon the instruments of the charge of their burden.

There are countless other examples that show us God is a master planner. Everything He has done and is doing has been well thought out and prepared. Often, Dr. Hutson would pose this question, "Has it ever occurred to you that nothing has ever occurred to God?" The whole universe steps in time to the music God composes. What an awesome thought —God is in control.

If we are to serve God effectively, we must seek to pattern after His methods. Everything we do in our service for Christ should be prayerfully planned and well prepared. We are instructed in I Corinthians 14:40, "Let all things be done decently and in order." For us to obey this directive, planning and preparation must come into play. The old saying, "To fail to plan is to plan to fail" is true, especially in our service for the Lord. In Luke 14:28-30, just several chapters before the steward's story is told, the principle of planning is illustrated: "For which of you, intending to build a tower, sitteth not down first, and counteth the cost, whether he have sufficient to finish it? Lest haply, after he hath laid the foundation, and is not able to finish it, all that behold it begin to mock him, Saying, this man began to build, and was not able to finish."

> *Many desire to do a great work for the Lord. The question is, "Do they have a plan, and are they prepared to accomplish the task?"*

In Luke 16, the steward demonstrated the power of effective planning and preparation. Knowing that his job was about to be terminated, he began to explore the possibilities of re-employment and prepared himself the best he could for what seemed inevitable in his future. Many desire to do a great work for the Lord. The question is, "Do they have a plan, and are they prepared to accomplish the task?" Nehemiah is perhaps the greatest book in the entire Bible on the subject of organizing a work for the Lord. The walls of Jerusalem symbolizing salvation and the gates symbolizing praise had laid in ruins one-hundred-sixty-one years before God raised up a man to organize the task of rebuilding. The massive task itself took only fifty-two days, but there were months of planning and preparation before the work ever started. It is amazing to see the prayerful planning that preceded this great victory for the people of God. Had Nehemiah showed up at Jerusalem with a burden, but no plan, this great work would have never been accomplished.

There are sincere workers of the Lord who will not go through the proper steps to prepare for the work they know the Lord has called them to do. It is wonderful to have zeal for the Lord, but that zeal needs to be coupled with knowledge and maturity that comes only through preparation. The methods may vary, but God always desires His servants to prepare for His work. This may be intensive years of training for a lifetime of ministry or simple week-to-week preparation for service in the local church.

The disciples of the Lord Jesus Christ seemed bewildered when their Master was crucified. Time and again the Lord had tried to prepare them by telling them that He would be killed and rise again on the third day (Matthew 16:21, 17:22-23). Even prophecy had foretold these events so clearly, but on the day of Jesus' resurrection we witness a scene of virtual panic. The narrative unfolds in John 20:1-22. Notice some of the highlights:

> The first day of the week cometh Mary Magdalene early, when it was yet dark, unto the sepulchre, and seeth the stone taken away from the sepulchre. Then she *runneth*, and cometh to Simon Peter, and to the other disciple, whom Jesus loved, and saith unto them, They have taken away the Lord out of the sepulchre, and we know not where they have laid him. Peter therefore went forth, and that other disciple, and came to the sepulchre. So they *ran* both together: and the other disciple did *outrun* Peter, and came first to the sepulchre [...]. For as yet they knew not the Scripture, that he must rise again from the dead. [...] Mary stood without at the sepulchre *weeping*: and as she *wept*, she stooped down, and looked into the sepulchre, and seeth two angels in white sitting, the one at the head, and the other at the feet, where the body of Jesus had lain. And they say unto her, Woman, why *weepest* thou? She saith unto them, Because they have taken away my Lord, and I know not where they have laid him [...]. Then the

same day at evening, being the first day of the week, when the doors were shut where the disciples were assembled for fear of the Jews, came Jesus and stood in the midst, and saith unto them, Peace be unto you. And when he had so said, he shewed unto them his hands and his side. Then were the disciples glad, when they saw the Lord. Then said Jesus to them again, Peace be unto you: as my Father hath sent me, even so send I you. And when he had said this, he breathed on them, and saith unto them, Receive ye the Holy Ghost.

Running and weeping among Jesus' disciples turned to rejoicing when Jesus opened their understanding. They had heard Him tell of His death and resurrection, but this truth did not register until they experienced this demonstration of God's power. Notice that after their zeal and compassion was balanced with the maturity of knowledge and experience, Jesus sent them forth to carry on His ministry. Their preparation of following the Lord, experiencing His power, and receiving the Holy Spirit qualified them for the ministry God had called them to.

> *Running and weeping among Jesus' disciples turned to rejoicing when Jesus opened their understanding.*

There are other workers for the Lord who believe it is somehow unspiritual to plan ahead. A church member, in all seriousness, once told me that he liked to think of himself as a leaf blowing in the wind. He couldn't make any plans, because he wanted to do whatever the Lord impressed on his heart. Evidently, there were some contrary winds that set him adrift. He sure blew around a lot, but interestingly enough, not by the church very often. I have met people who feel they should not write out an order of worship, organize programs, or plan visitation. Others take it a step further by not even studying to teach or preach. I do not doubt the sincerity of their heart; in fact, I am quick to defend their motives. They have a definite desire to allow the Holy Spirit to lead their service for Christ, but in their zeal for the Lord they have missed a fundamental principle. The consequence is haphazard, ineffective work that brings about few results.

The problems outlined above are present, but not nearly as prevalent in our day as pure, simple lack of commitment and dedication. These believers understand the importance of planning and preparation, but are increasingly unconcerned about the kingdom of God and it shows in the quality of their service. There are two distinct possibilities. Perhaps hearts are cold, indifferent, and out of fellowship with God. On the other hand, it is possible that hearts are right, but people have grown lax. We are in a consumer-driven society where people are conditioned to look more for what God can do for them, rather than look for what they can do for God.

There is another group of willing people who want to do a good job for the Lord, but have not been trained properly. Whatever the reason, there is an appalling lack of preparation in our service for the Lord. It is important to allow the Holy Spirit to guide, but He readily will do so as we plan and prepare. Even after careful planning, there will be times He will change our entire plan, up to the last minute before work begins—sometimes even during our work. We must remain flexible to His leading, but careful planning and preparation will accomplish much more for the cause of Christ. Consider this epitaph inscribed by God about an Old Testament king, "So Jotham became mighty, because he prepared his ways before the LORD his God" (II Chronicles 27:6).

Before getting into the specific steps of planning and preparation found in the next several chapters, some basics must be addressed. First of all, a person should only plan and prepare for their area of responsibility within positional structure. No work for the Lord should be attempted without divine sanctioning. Second, a person's heart must be in tune with the Lord, fully surrendered to His guidance. Third, all efforts will be completely futile unless they are surrounded by prayer. Our time of planning is seeking God's wisdom and leading concerning specific requests, made in light of duties He has laid upon our hearts to perform. The work is the Lord's and anything accomplished will be because He works in us and through us, allowing us to work alongside Him in His master plan.

How important it is to develop a plan, and prepare for opportunities that God may bring your way. In Genesis 24 we are told the wonderful story of a bride being chosen for Isaac. Abraham sent his servant, Eliezer, some four hundred and thirty miles back to his homeland in search of a bride whom God would choose. Upon arriving, Eliezer prayed God would have His choice of a bride reveal herself by offering to draw water for his camels in response to a request for a drink for himself. It wasn't long before Rebekah came to draw water and fulfilled the prayer of the servant. After the camels were watered, Eliezer gave her gifts and asked if there was room for him and his traveling companions to lodge at her father's house. She immediately invited them to stay. Leaving him by the well she ran home and hastily told her family about the guest. Her brother, Laban, ran right out to the well and invited the Eliezer to come in, making an astounding statement, "I have prepared the house, and room for the camels" (Genesis 24:31). Now when would he have had time to make the preparations? It appears that he was already prepared. What a wonderful truth is presented here; had Rebekah's family not been prepared, they just might have missed the blessings of God.

Another interesting facet in this same story is the statement made by Eliezer, "I being in the way, the LORD led me" (Genesis 24:27). Abraham's preparation and planning resulted in Eliezer being led by the Lord to His choice of a bride for Isaac. Without a plan, without any preparation, there would not have been God's choice of a bride for Isaac.

Prayerful planning and preparation places a person in a position of availability for God's provision of possibilities; thereby enabling that person to increase his or her productivity in the cause of Christ.

CHAPTER SEVEN

Determining Your Goal

The steward of Luke 16 was not floating through life, content to stumble across whatever came into his path. He had a very definite goal to become re-employed in a similar or better position than he had. This goal was the motivation for the plan he devised and the driving force behind the preparation that was made.

Do you remember the old cliché: "If you aim at nothing, that is what you will hit every time." If you set out to work with no real goal in mind, how can you expect to accomplish anything at all? An elderly gentleman was driving along a major highway after dark, inside a large metropolitan area. He was taking his family to town for a special event. Traffic was especially heavy and he hunched over the steering wheel, tightly gripping it with both hands. Cars darted around him and brake lights flashed in the irregular pattern of big-city traffic. Tension mounted inside the car as the passengers tried to remain calm in spite of several near-collisions. Finally, after struggling to contain herself, his wife blurted out her advice,

"Be careful of that car up ahead!" The man in all seriousness responded, "Honey, I don't know what I'm doing; I don't know where I'm at; and I don't know where I'm going; but, if you don't hush and leave me alone you are going to mess me up." Sadly, many people never seem to know where they are going and for that reason never accomplish a whole lot.

Setting the Goal

A goal keeps you focused on the finish line, which in turn keeps you functioning in the midst of frustration. Jesus' experience while on earth is an inspiring legacy of what can be endured and accomplished while working a plan to fulfill a certain goal. God's entire objective in sending His only begotten Son into a sin-cursed world was to reconcile mankind to Himself. He accomplished this by providing them a way of escape from punishment. John 3:16-17 gives us a glimpse into the mind of God, "For God so loved the world, that he gave his only begotten Son, that whosoever believeth in him should not perish, but have everlasting life. For God sent not his Son into the world to condemn the world; but that the world through him might be saved." This master plan was put in motion by the coming of Jesus to the earth. There was a thirty-three year span of time from His birth until His ascension to the Father. During this interval, Jesus faced many frustrations. What kept Him functioning was the goal the Father had given Him. Look at Hebrews 12:2, "Looking unto Jesus the author and finisher of our faith; who for the joy that was set before him endured the cross, despising the shame, and is set down at the right hand of the throne of God."

> *All planning and preparation must be defined, molded, and evaluated based on its compliance with meeting our bottom line.*

So, you have to have a bottom line. In the business world, the bottom line is obvious. There is creative packaging to communicate the goal, but anybody who knows business understands monetary gain is of utmost importance. There are different strategies employed. For instance, large corporations sometimes invest heavily in what may appear to be a losing proposition. However, you can rest assured the tax benefits or future earnings far outweigh any losses—at least in theory. The approach differs, but all business strategy and decisions must square with the bottom line.

In Luke 16:9 Jesus defines the ultimate goal for all believers, "Make to yourselves friends of the mammon of unrighteousness; that, when ye fail, they may receive you into everlasting habitations." We are to use earthly means to win precious souls to the Saviour, thereby building the kingdom of God. All planning and preparation must be defined, molded, and evaluated based on its compliance with meeting our bottom line.

Many believers have never done much for God. Upon examination of their goals the reason is apparent: sadly, the kingdom of God does not come first in their lives. Instead, they determine in their hearts to seek fulfillment through obtaining the things of this world. With this being their goal, they spend most of their time pursuing worldly treasure, leaving God their leftover time, if any at all. Dr. Millard J. Erickson, in a discussion on "The Christian View of Humanity" from his book *Christian Theology*, lends the following advice:

> We cannot discover our real meaning by regarding ourselves and our own happiness as the highest of all values, nor find happiness, fulfillment, or satisfaction by seeking it directly. Our value has been conferred on us by a higher source, and we are fulfilled only when serving and loving that higher being. It is then that satisfaction comes, as a by-product of commitment to God. It is then that we realize the truth of Jesus' statement, "For whosoever will save his life shall lose it; but whosoever shall lose his life for my sake and the gospel's, the same shall save it" (Mark 8:35).[8]

Wouldn't it be better for these believers, who have never done much for God, to reprioritize; thereby investing their life in the cause of Christ with an ultimate goal to serve Him? The way to fulfillment is following Jesus' command, "Seek ye first the kingdom of God, and his righteousness; and all these things shall be added unto you" (Matthew 6:33).

Other believers start out to do a great work for God, but easily give up when trouble comes. This can be traced to their lack of ability to see things the way God sees them. Remember Hebrews 12:2? This passage tells us that the goal Jesus' Father had given Him kept Him functioning through the frustrations of the cross. Hebrews 12:3-4 goes on to say, "For consider him that endured such contradiction of sinners against himself, lest ye be wearied and faint in your minds. Ye have not yet resisted unto blood, striving against sin." When we are saved by the marvelous grace of the Lord Jesus Christ, we enter into a spiritual warfare. Where once we walked the path of sin in step with the world, we now have turned and are walking against the flow of this world. Jesus gave His life in cruel death on the cross that we might be victorious in our battle. What a source of encouragement it is to consider the price He paid. How this ought to motivate us to stay faithful as we look toward the final result of the work He has called us to do. "Therefore, my beloved brethren, be ye steadfast, unmoveable, always abounding in the work of the Lord, forasmuch as ye know that your labour is not in vain in the Lord" (I Corinthians 15:58).

Setting Targeted Objectives

Having determined our goal in a general way, we then must decide specifically, with the Lord's leading, how to go about meeting that goal by setting targeted objectives. Everyone will not be saved through door-to-door visitation, but many have been. Everyone will not be saved through pulpit preaching, but many have been. Everyone will not be saved through Sunday School teaching, but many have been. Everyone will not be saved through gospel singing, but some have been. Everyone will not be saved through church fellowship socials, but a few have been. We could go on and on. The Lord uses a variety of ways to reach the lost. Also, it must be pointed out that unless the saved are discipled and ministered to, they will be unable to reach others. God uses a variety of ministries in different ways to accomplish His ultimate goal. More importantly, decide what God would have you to do and then determine in your heart to place all your efforts in that ministry, with an ultimate goal of introducing the lost to the Saviour.

> *God has called upon some to finance the work of the Lord. These individuals are especially gifted to generate cash flow and are called upon to invest heavily in the work of Christ.*

Along these lines, there is an area that should be covered. God has called upon some to finance the work of the Lord. These individuals are especially gifted to generate cash flow and are called upon to invest heavily in the work of Christ. This is a vital ingredient to the success of building the Kingdom. If this is the case, these individuals will view money as a tool and leverage all the weight they can by giving strategically, as they are led of the Lord, to ministries that are carrying forth the light of the precious gospel of Christ. May God increase the number of people called and dedicated to the task of providing material means to accomplish the Heavenly goal; however, before leaving this subject, several words of caution should be mentioned.

First of all, this calling should not interfere with "reasonable service" (Romans 12:1-2) expected of every believer in the local church. Secondly, someone who believes he is being led to finance the work of the Lord must cautiously examine his heart to be certain that he is not "buying his way out" of service for Christ, but is actually serving Christ in His calling to raise finances to proliferate the gospel. This person's deep, underlying motive should not be personal position or prosperity, but prosperity and prominence of the mission: "Make to yourselves friends of the *mammon of unrighteousness* (using earthly means); that, when ye fail, they may receive you into everlasting habitations" (Luke 16:9).

Who Needs My Ministry?

The first question to ask when determining a specific objective is, "Who needs my ministry?" You can never set an effective objective until you have answered this question. You must determine if your ministry is a valid concept—is there really a need it will fill? If so, who is my target group? Sadly, most churches never understand the spiritual condition of their community. Christians somehow miss the truth that most in their community are not on their way to Heaven. It will help us to effectively plan if we know who we are trying to reach. For example, an eighth grade Sunday School teacher should look around the community identifying eighth graders. How many eighth graders live within five miles of the church? Ten miles? Fifteen miles? How many of these teenagers are unchurched?

What Are Their Needs?

The second question to pose, "What are their needs?" A valid ministry must reach people, and to reach people you must connect with them. This involves understanding them enough to devise a plan that meets their specific needs. People gravitate to a source that meets a need in their life. At this point, one must take inventory of the situation, as it really is, for the group they are trying to reach. You must enter into their world. Look at the pressures they face. Find out what it would take to make a difference. All of this information will help to create a burden in your heart for the people God would have you reach, while shaping objectives that govern your operation.

A preacher should not preach without first gaining insight to the congregation that will hear the message. A music director should not select music without understanding the congregation that will sing and listen. We could go on and on. You are not connecting with people until you are meeting their needs. For example, the same eighth grade Sunday School teacher should start to learn about the needs of eighth-graders. What do they like or dislike? What is their home life like? How do they feel about their friends? What mistakes are they making? What changes are taking place in their life? What are they learning in school? How much do they know about the Bible? Do they know Jesus?

How Will They Be Contacted?

Thirdly, "How will they be contacted?" A plan must be devised that puts you in touch with the people who need your ministry. By now you know who they are, what their needs are, and you have developed a plan to meet those needs. All this is just an idea unless it becomes reality by actually *reaching* the targeted group. A plan must be devised to penetrate the group the Lord has laid on your heart. So many ministries fall short in this area. There are some wonderful programs out there that really meet needs. Many would get saved, if only the message got out to more people. Many churches are located in the heart of a busy city; they have a pastor who preaches the gospel every service, yet few are being saved.

The problem is not with the church understanding who needs their ministry—everyone has the basic need of salvation. The problem is not with the church meeting their needs, for the church has wonderful programs to do just that. The problem may be that the church is not contacting the people who need their help. Any business knows that if it sits back and waits for people to come to them, it won't be long until they will go out of business. There are a few exceptions to this rule because of a unique business, but there are no exceptions to the rule of reaching people given to us by Jesus himself, "Go out into the highways and hedges, and compel them to come in, that my house may be filled" (Luke 14:23).

Returning to our example, the Sunday school teacher must find out how to get in touch with all the eighth graders in the area. Should he devise special activities that would interest them? Could he volunteer at a local school? Attend junior high athletic events? Somehow, this teacher must plan a way to get in contact with eighth graders.

How Will Success Be Evaluated?

The last question to complete this process is, "How will success be evaluated?" In order to stay motivated there must be some system of accountability built into your plan. This allows you to adjust your plan and prepare for effectiveness in the future. You need to know when your objective has been achieved. This will inspire you to set a new objective and adjust your thinking to the ever-changing demands of your ministry. Planning and preparation is a never-ending process that must be prayerfully evaluated in an ongoing way.

In Conclusion

As you determine your objectives, look down the road. Of course, only God knows the future and a person surrendered to His will give Him complete liberty to lead wherever He desires. This is the Lord's work; however, we should be in a position to be blessed and increased if that is His desire. There are some things in life on which one should not economize, and one of those things is the scope of God's design. Make certain you do not limit God with a lack of faith. As you look down the road, ask yourself the following question: "Where do we need to go, and what will it take to get there?" Most folks can barely see to the end of a week; others, a few weeks or months ahead. But it takes people of real vision and faith to put themselves in a position of availability for what they believe God would have them do years down the road.

You must have a purpose—an objective. The great evangelist Billy Sunday (1862–1935) once said, "More men fail through lack of purpose than through lack of talent."[9] Billy Sunday's life story is one of success—not only in the world, but more importantly in the kingdom of God. Although reared in an orphanage, by the age of twenty-one he was playing professional baseball for the Chicago White Sox.[10] Three years later he was gloriously saved at the Pacific Garden Rescue Mission. In his own words he describes what took place:

> I arose and said to the boys [teammates], 'I'm through. I am going to Jesus Christ. We've come to the parting of the ways,' and I turned my back on them. [. . .] I turned and left that little group on the corner of State and Madison Streets and walked to the little mission and fell on my knees and staggered out of sin and into the arms of the Saviour.[11]

Five years after his salvation, he gave up baseball, responding to the calling of God to preach. He determined, "I want to be a giant for God,"[12] and he was just that! In Philadelphia alone, over two million, three hundred thousand people attended during the seventy-eight days of his campaign. Of these, it is reported that 41,724 publicly trusted Christ as their Saviour.[13] Throughout his ministry, hundreds of thousands responded to his public invitations to receive Christ, "hitting the sawdust trail"[14] to clasp his hand, signifying their acceptance of Christ.

How we need to purpose in our hearts! We have a goal, which must be recognized and embraced. Then objectives should be set in order to reach our goal. When we have done these things, we are not guaranteed success; however, not doing so does guarantee failure. Set your sights, trim your sails, and be ready for God to thrust you forward in your service for Him.

> *When we have done these things, we are not guaranteed success; however, not doing so does guarantee failure.*

CHAPTER EIGHT

Envisioning Obstacles

The unjust steward had enough forethought and wisdom to skirt disaster by preparing for the inevitable. At a time when most would worry about the past; bottling themselves up in discouragement by dwelling on what might have been; this man developed a strategy for his future. There were substantial obstacles barring success, but he embraced the situation he could not change, making the negatives work in his favor to accomplish his goal. A great principle emerges from the action of this unjust steward: take every situation that seems negative and look for ways to make something positive out of it.

A successful business man, Michael Kewer, cites the following philosophy, which his company operates with: "*Negative* becomes *challenge*—we do not even use the word 'negative' to describe a situation; instead we choose to think of it as a 'challenging' situation. You can draw something positive out of any situation and although you can't change everything, you can change a portion of the situation and make things work in your direction." Obstacles can be roadblocks or stepping-stones depending on the effectiveness of your planning and preparation. I'll never forget a customer calling the office one day to file a complaint. She claimed the agent handling her rental did not know what he was doing, making the process take far too long. She described the situation, finally coming to this conclusion, "Sir, I'm sorry to say this, but your agent is just a 'duck.'" I told her I did not understand. She went on to explain, "You see there are two types of people in this world, 'ducks' and 'eagles.' He does a great job until he has to handle something out of the ordinary. Then he just sits there like a duck that swam into something on the lake—not knowing how to get around it. If he were like an eagle, he would just spread his wings and fly over or around it."

There have been many people who have set out to serve God with a wonderful goal in mind. There was nothing wrong with their purpose or their plan. The problem surfaced when they ran into obstacles they did not know how to handle. Take time as you prepare to envision the obstacles you will face. Once you identify the possible obstacles, devise a plan to overcome them. You will find that effective, prayerful planning prevents most problems. Dr. Curtis Hutson used to say, "If you are chopping down trees, taking time out to sharpen your axe is never wasted time." The time you spend "sharpening your axe" will tremendously help when the obstacles surface. There are four areas you should consider as you devise a plan to handle these pending obstacles:

Resources

First of all, you need to evaluate your resources. The steward was up against a huge roadblock. A devastating audit was in progress that would result in termination of his employment. This would ravage his resumé. What would he do without a favorable recommendation? So he thought to himself, "What is available that I have not put to use in my favor?" He evaluated his resources, realizing he still had influence over his owner's accounts. This he put to work overcoming the obstacle of a poor recommendation.

Ask yourself, "What is on hand that we are not using?" Many times the solution to the problem is already within your grasp. There is no reason to "re-invent the wheel." Take your resources and put them to work. In order to be truly objective in your evaluation you must have a good understanding of your team. What are their abilities? Training? Education?

If there is no resource on hand to address the obstacle, you then ask yourself, "What else is out there?" A body of water that has no inflow or outflow becomes stagnant. Many never get past hurdles because they refuse to tap into resources beyond what they have on hand. Look around and see who you can recruit. What kind of training can you get for yourself and your team? What products have been developed that will make you more effective?

Priorities

Second, employ age-old wisdom—divide and conquer. You eat a pie one slice at a time and you build a work for God one step at a time. "Rome was not built in a day"; in fact, any worthwhile work will not materialize overnight. So, pace yourself for the long haul. The Christian life is not a sprint race; it is a marathon. When you begin to envision the obstacles, the list may grow enormously. We have a real enemy—Satan. He brings all the opposition he can muster when a believer honestly, wholeheartedly seeks to do a work for God. Mrs. John R. Rice used to tell us, "If it were easy to serve God, everybody would be doing it!" How will you deal with all the possible obstacles and not be overwhelmed?

> *The Christian life is not a sprint race; it is a marathon.*

For instance, suppose the Lord has called you to be a missionary to Japan. Without a whole lot of thought we can list quite a few obstacles. How will you raise financial support? How will you learn the language? What about the culture shock? Where will you live? How will the children see the grandparents? Where will they go to school? How will you establish a local church? How will you train a national pastor? Where will you get supplies? And the list goes on and on. . .

Your best line of defense is to prioritize. Since you cannot accomplish all these things within your first year, you will have to decide what is most important. That is the place you will start. That does not mean you will not accomplish your entire goal, but simply you will work on the obstacles one at a time, in order of importance.

Change

But, what about obstacles which seem unconquerable? You hit a wall that seems insurmountable. That is when you must look for a fresh approach—you may have to *change*. As painful as that is for some, it is necessary to overcome obstacles. For some reason, in the ministry it is hard to change methods. We would rather sit like a duck on a pond than spread our wings and chart a new course! We get "stuck in a rut" so easily. It would help us to venture along new paths as we conquer obstacles for Jesus' sake! For the sake of clarity, we are not talking about changing the Bible or fundamental doctrine. No, no! That is timeless truth that transcends all boundaries. We are simply suggesting change in our methods. In the early days of our country, during the French and Indian War, the French and colonists were not making any headway as long as they fought in true European style. Finally, they realized that to fight Indians they would have to fight *like* Indians. They changed history when they changed their methods to meet the cunning of their enemy.

We must be willing to try a fresh approach. Along these lines, you must keep brainstorming until you hit upon something that will work. We should not give up in despair; we have already been promised the victory. I John 5:4 says, "For whatsoever is born of God overcometh the world: and this is the victory that overcometh the world, even our faith." Romans 8:31 reminds us of a wonderful truth, "What shall we then say to these things? If God be for us, who can be against us?" We are on the winning side when we are operating in the will of God, with a desire to do a work for Him. Take it to the Lord in prayer and keep praying until the Lord gives you the key that will unlock the door, conquering the obstacle.

A man once told me, "You are either a 'thermometer' or a 'thermostat.' You either register what the conditions are or you set out to change the conditions." Don't be a "thermometer." There are plenty of believers who can describe in detail the obstacles that are hindering the work of God, but there are few that can provide solutions that will work. Be a "thermostat" and turn up the heat for God. Make an impact in the area God has entrusted to your care. "But they that wait upon the LORD shall renew their strength; they shall mount up with wings as eagles; they shall run, and not be weary; and they shall walk, and not faint" (Isaiah 40:31).

Boundaries

In order to overcome some obstacles, a third method must be employed: set boundaries. There has never been a successful organization that has been able to operate without some rules. The work of God is no exception. The Apostle Paul admonished Titus, "For this cause left I thee in Crete, that thou shouldest set in order the things that are wanting [. . .]." His reasoning was clear, "For there are many unruly and vain talkers and deceivers, specially they of the circumcision: whose mouths must be stopped, who subvert whole houses, teaching things which they ought not [. . .]. Wherefore rebuke them sharply, that they may be sound in the faith" (Titus 1:5, 10-11, 13). Paul also warned the Corinthian church, "[. . .] The rest will I set in order when I come" (I Corinthians 11:34). Well-defined boundaries protect the integrity of the organization, keeping obstacles from becoming spectacles.

Many of our boundaries come directly out of Scripture. However, many times practical rules must be developed that fine-tune Biblical, broad-based boundaries for specific applications. When setting up rules, the following things should be kept in mind:

- Make rules clear and simple.
- Make rules somewhat flexible.
- Make rules enforceable.

> *It would be better to have fewer rules and have them followed than to have so many rules that no one can remember them.*

Your rules will not be of any help unless the people they protect can understand and remember them. It would be better to have fewer rules and have them followed than to have so many rules that no one can remember them. In like respect, rules must be communicated. For example, if God has called you to work with children, you can't allow several children to spoil the entire class because of their misbehavior. It would be foolish to have an elaborate set of rules and regulations governing when they can go to the bathroom, when they can stand, sit, talk, etc... It would be better to have several clear, simple rules like "no talking when the teacher is talking," "do not get out of your seat without permission," and "raise your hand if you have a question."

The rules you make should be somewhat flexible. Be careful of using the words "must," "always," and "never." A rule that does not bend will probably break. Don't give the situation you are trying to control a chance to control you by putting yourself into a corner. Make the rules flexible enough that you can decide where to draw the line without putting yourself into a win or lose conflict. In addition, make the rules adaptable for growth and change. The answer some people have to every obstacle is to make a new rule. If your rules are flexible enough, you will find they will adapt to most situations.

The rules you set will have to be enforceable. What good is a rule that you can't enforce? No matter how clear, simple, or flexible your rules are, someone will challenge your authority. When that happens, you must be prepared to resolutely take a stand and enforce the rule. If you are unable to enforce the rule, your authority will be severely compromised and any respect you have fostered will be lost.

When I was a youth minister we ran activities on these simple, clear rules given at the start of every activity:

- Stay with the group.
- Follow any directions given to you by an adult with the group.
- Remember you are with a church group, so please act accordingly.

We would then go on to tell them that we certainly wanted them to have a good time, but for their protection and ours, these simple rules would have to be enforced. The consequence was then made very clear, "If you break these rules, your parents will be called to come for you." We had very few problems, even with the toughest kids.

In Conclusion

To wrap up this matter, you can never predict all the obstacles you may face, but you will be amazed how accurate you will be with the guidance of the Holy Spirit and the counsel of people who have experience in your area. When an obstacle surfaces that you had not expected, the preparation of your heart will help you adjust to the new challenge more readily. The Scripture teaches, "For God is not the author of confusion, but of peace, as in all churches of the saints" (I Corinthians 14:33). We see in God's plan for mankind that there is not an obstacle that can surface that God hasn't already put a plan in place to provide a solution. What a wonderful Designer!

CHAPTER NINE

Organizing Your Thoughts

Now that you have determined your goal and envisioned the obstacles—devising a plan to overcome them, you need to organize your thoughts by writing out a plan of action. You need a written plan to get you from where you are now to where you need to be. Our Lord gives us instruction in Habakkuk 2:2-4:

> 2 And the LORD answered me, and said, Write the vision, and make it plain upon tables, that he may run that readeth it.
>
> 3 For the vision is yet for an appointed time, but at the end it shall speak, and not lie: though it tarry, wait for it; because it will surely come, it will not tarry.
>
> 4 Behold, his soul which is lifted up is not upright in him: but the just shall live by his faith.

Notice the wording of verse two. It does not say, "So he that runneth may read," as you would expect if it were speaking of a messenger carrying a message. But the wording is, "that he may run that readeth it!"15 Literally, the prophet was admonished to make the plan so clear that once a person read it, he or she would be able to adopt the plan—putting it into action.

A clearly written plan is the first step of good communication. Your plan should be well thought out and written so clearly that it can readily be put in motion. As you write out your plan, include steps and target dates. Where do you want to be and when do you need to be there? You have divided up the task and prioritized. Now is the time to assign a time frame to each category. This will help to keep you focused in the days ahead. Just because you are not doing everything that needs to be done right now, the last thing you want to do is forget where you are going, or "settle in" before you make it to the destination. This written plan is a tool that you will refer to often in the days ahead as you evaluate your effectiveness for the Lord.

Most importantly, notice Habakkuk 2:4, "[. . .] The just shall live by his faith." You must keep your plan of action in perspective. It is only a guideline that is to be spoken of by faith, believing God has given the vision to you. "For now we see through a glass, darkly; but then face to face: now I know in part; but then shall I know even as also I am known" (I Corinthians 13:12). We do have limited vision, and because of this our written plan will have to be adjusted as we go along.

If you are under another's leadership, you will want and need his approval before implementing your ideas. So, after your plan is well thought out and written, meet with your leader for his input and changes that he may feel are necessary. There are several reasons this meeting will be of mutual benefit.

First of all, this respects his leadership and responsibility over your area. Ultimately, your leader is responsible for the success of your plan so he should be included in its design.

Secondly, this is a safeguard for you—it keeps you from being a lone-ranger out on the wide-open prairie with no support. For a plan to come together and be successful, you will need support from the person above you. If you launch a program without his understanding and blessing, you will have a difficult time mobilizing and equipping a workforce. What is a coach with no football team; or, a band director without a band?

Thirdly, this meeting taps into your leader's wisdom and experience. He is probably a leader for a good reason. As you lay out your plan of action, you will be amazed at the insight he will have. He may be able to identify potential problems that you have overlooked, giving you a chance to solve them before your plan is implemented.

Lastly, you need to make certain you are on the same page—heading the same direction as the leader that God has placed over you. Although you may have a wonderful plan, you may find out he desires to go in a slightly different direction, for the time being. It would be foolish to launch a plan, only to have your leader launch something else along the same lines—splitting the focus of the people burdened about your area. People working together in unity can accomplish so much more. The goal being reached is of primary importance! Plans and methods can always be negotiated, as long as the purpose of the organization is not compromised.

Once you have written your final plan, be certain you have not overlooked an avenue of opportunity. In our text, Luke 16, do you see the diversity of the steward's plan? Look at verse five more closely: "So he called every one of his lord's debtors unto him [. . .]." Remember his goal? He needed one job—just one! But he investigated every single area of opportunity available to him. He was not content to "put all his eggs in one basket." He increased his chances of success with every contact that he made.

Like the steward, diversify. Drop a line in every pond that has fish and you will catch more fish. Don't change your ultimate goal, but look for more than just one way to accomplish it. The caution is against becoming so focused on your plan that you ignore other opportunities that may speed you on to your destination.

> *Like the steward, diversify. Drop a line in every pond that has fish and you will catch more fish. Don't change your ultimate goal, but look for more than just one way to accomplish it.*

I remember when we took on the challenge of planting a church. We were in the midst of a growing town with no permanent church building, struggling to get together a group of people to attend the new church. We had secured permission to conduct services in the cafeteria of the middle school and had gathered together about ten families. We were following my carefully thought-out plan of evangelism and had been successful in getting several of the new believers to help in the effort. One gentleman, not real keen on the plan, approached me with a plan of his own. He had put considerable thought into his idea that probably would have accomplished a similar objective. I quickly excused his idea, explaining that with so few people we needed to focus all of our attention on the plan we had been using. In result, he quit helping us with evangelism altogether. Had I adopted his plan—alongside of my plan, he probably would have headed it up and recruited an entire separate staff of workers, resulting in more people saved, baptized, and added to the church.

Be careful of becoming so organized and "programmed" that you are not open to availing yourself of opportunities the Lord may bring your way.

While still in the planning and preparation stage, be sure you have taken time to think your plan all the way through to the end. Be diligent enough to go back, rethink, and pray over every step that you have laid out. Don't be afraid to rewrite your plan over and over again. Colossians 3:15 admonishes us, "Let the peace of God rule in your hearts [. . .]." If there is caution in your heart, keep working on the plan and praying over it until you and your leader have perfect peace about the direction you intend to pursue. This will help you succeed when you put things in motion.

CHAPTER TEN

The Most Important Plan of All

Have you ever paused to consider the emptiness of life? I challenge you to take a few moments and allow your mind to travel back in time over the past week, the past month, and even the past year, answering the following questions: "What have you done that has made a lasting contribution?" "What has truly been accomplished?" "What is really going to survive your existence on this earth?" "Is there meaning for your labor?" These questions and many like them can be troubling as you search for answers that will validate the impression you have made on this earth.

It was said of Alexander the Great that he conquered all of his known world. While at the pinnacle of this success, history records that he wept and said, "There are no more worlds to conquer." What a sad reality: a man of his prominence and seeming success left behind a self-inscribed legacy of dissatisfaction and emptiness.

King Solomon had everything that an imagination could long for. He lived in great palaces complete with orchards, vineyards, and beautiful gardens. His unsurpassed wisdom and knowledge coupled with his position and fame made him one of the most sought after men of his day. His band of loyal servants stood ready to bring his every wish into reality. He accumulated wealth and riches unspeakable, insomuch that he was able to say, "Whatsoever my eyes desired I kept not from them. I withheld not my heart from any joy" (Ecclesiastes 2:10). Yet even he, toward the end of his life, surveyed all of these accomplishments -along with everything that he had—and made this tremendous statement: "All is vanity and vexation of spirit, and there is no profit under the sun" (Ecclesiastes 2:11). Literally, Solomon sharing from his heart said that everything he had done was meaningless and empty. It was as if he had been chasing the wind, grasping for contentment, and yet never obtaining a real purpose for his existence. With a sense of hopelessness he concludes that nothing of real, lasting value had been accomplished because of his life.

> *There is an unavoidable reality of an appointed death for every mortal.*

All of the great men and women of the past have one thing in common. Although the epitaph inscribed on their tombstone varies, lauding the accomplishments of their life; inscribed beneath these memorable words is a date of birth and yes, sadly, a date of death. There is an unavoidable reality of an appointed death for every mortal.

The Apostle Paul must have grasped this truth for he exclaimed, "If in this life only we have hope in Christ, we are of all men most miserable" (I Corinthians 15:19). So, what profit is there in life? Nothing really satisfies. Not much of what we do survives the grave. Life really is empty. It seems we wake in the morning, prepare for the day, only to repeat the process the next day with very little in between that brings lasting satisfaction. We make money, only to have it vanish with the high cost of living and inflation. We eat a meal, only to be hungry again hours later. We quench our thirst, only to be thirsty again. We exercise to become fit, only to experience disease or other physical complications for which we are not prepared.

No wonder the suicide rate among young people is on the rise. Is life just a vicious cycle? Is there really something to fill this emptiness in life? In answer to these questions we turn our thoughts to Isaiah 55:

1 Ho, every one that thirsteth, come ye to the waters, and he that hath no money; come ye, buy, and eat; yea, come, buy wine and milk without money and without price.

2 Wherefore do ye spend money for that which is not bread? And your labour for that which satisfieth not? Hearken diligently unto me, and eat ye that which is good, and let your soul delight itself in fatness.

3 Incline your ear, and come unto me: hear, and your soul shall live; and I will make an everlasting covenant with you, even the sure mercies of David.

4 Behold, I have given him for a witness to the people, a leader and commander to the people.

5 Behold, thou shalt call a nation that thou knowest not, and nations that knew not thee shall run unto thee because of the LORD thy God, and for the Holy One of Israel; for he hath glorified thee.

6 Seek ye the LORD while he may be found, call ye upon him while he is near:

7 Let the wicked forsake his way, and the unrighteous man his thoughts: and let him return unto the LORD, and he will have mercy upon him; and to our God, for he will abundantly pardon.

8 For my thoughts are not your thoughts, neither are your ways my ways, saith the LORD.

9 For as the heavens are higher than the earth, so are my ways higher than your ways, and my thoughts than your thoughts.

10 For as the rain cometh down, and the snow from heaven, and returneth not thither, but watereth the earth, and maketh it bring forth and bud, that it may give seed to the sower, and bread to the eater:

11 So shall my word be that goeth forth out of my mouth: it shall not return unto me void, but it shall accomplish that which I please, and it shall prosper in the thing whereto I sent it.

12 For ye shall go out with joy, and be led forth with peace: the mountains and the hills shall break forth before you into singing, and all the trees of the field shall clap their hands.

13 Instead of the thorn shall come up the fir tree, and instead of the brier shall come up the myrtle tree: and it shall be to the LORD for a name, for an everlasting sign that shall not be cut off.

To have an understanding of this passage, we must first examine the concept of a soul, introduced in verses two and three above. The "soul" is the essence of life. The inner person is to be distinguished from the outer person, or what we refer to as the "body." The possession of a soul is unique to mankind and differentiates us from all other life forms created by God. The Scripture teaches in Genesis 1:27, "God created man in His own image; in the image of God created He him." The Scripture goes on to explain in Genesis 2:7, "The Lord God formed man out of the dust of the ground and breathed into his nostrils the breath of life; and man became a living soul." Notice that the body, the outer man, was created from the dust of the ground. However, the soul was implanted into man as a direct gift from God and is what makes us a spiritual being. God desires fellowship with mankind, therefore He has entrusted to us a soul that can communicate with Him. Beyond decay of the mortal body, our soul will live on for eternity to be reunited with its resurrected body one day.

> *The Scripture makes clear that if we die in our sin we are alienated from God...*

In the original state of creation, Adam and Eve enjoyed this fellowship with God without any barriers to impede their communication. This continued until the day they chose to disobey His command and partake of the forbidden fruit. The consequence of this sin was spiritual death, which alienated their souls from God—thus breaking their fellowship.

Romans 5:12 explains how their disobedience is relevant to us: "Wherefore as by one man [Adam] sin entered into the world, and death by sin, and so death passed upon all men, for that all have sinned." Universally, we are born into this world with an inherited, sinful nature. Psalms 53:2-3 says, "God looked down from heaven upon the children of men, to see if there were any that did understand, that did seek God. Every one of them is gone back: they are altogether become filthy; there is none that doeth good, no, not one." With this inherited nature comes the inherited consequence: spiritual death and eternal separation from God. Isaiah 59:2 informs us: "Your iniquities have separated between you and your God, and your sins have hid His face from you that He will not hear." The Scripture makes clear that if we die in our sin we are alienated from God and we spend eternity in a place the Bible calls "Hell." This verse explains, "In flaming fire taking vengeance on them that know not God and that obey not the gospel of our Lord Jesus Christ; who shall be punished with everlasting destruction from the presence of the Lord and from the glory of His power" (II Thessalonians 1:8-9).

When we understand that we have an eternal soul that has been cut off from God by sin, a natural response is to try and make up for past failures. Many vow to turn over a new leaf and set out to try to do the right things in their life. They may join a church, become a better neighbor, or try to curb bad habits to somehow gain favor with God against whom they have sinned. But a problem with that approach is brought to the surface in Isaiah 64:6: "But we are all as an unclean thing, and all our righteousnesses are as filthy rags; and we all do fade as a leaf; and our iniquities [sin], like the wind, have taken us away."

Look at the illustration above in Isaiah 64:6. Our life is compared to the life of a leaf. A leaf lives because it is attached to its source of life, the tree. During the autumn season the leaves begin to fade: first changing color, then dropping to the ground, and then they are carried away from the tree by the wind. It is during this season of the year that we admire the beauty of the leaves the most; when in reality they are in a state of death. Scientists tell us that this process of fading occurs because a valve in the stem of the leaf closes with the changing of the weather, cutting the leaf off from its source of life, the tree. Because of this, the leaf no longer receives nutrients from the tree. This causes the leaf to begin the process of death, ultimately leading to its complete destruction. How foolish it would be for us to gather up leaves that have fallen from a tree and try to transplant them, water them, or even fertilize them, hoping to bring them back to life. Obviously, that would not solve the basic problem of the leaf; it would do nothing to impede its deteriorating process.

> *We have been cut off from God, because of our sin and until that barrier is removed, nothing we do will make any difference in our eternal destination.*

Likewise, it is foolish to think that good works or righteous deeds make up for sin and somehow gain favor with God. We have been cut off from God, because of our sin and until that barrier is removed, nothing we do will make any difference in our eternal destination. Isaiah 64:7 is quick to remind us that we are, within ourselves, hopelessly separated from God. "And there is none that calleth upon thy name, that stirreth up himself to take hold of thee: for thou hast hid thy face from us, and hast consumed us, because of our iniquities."

An Intriguing Invitation

Set against this backdrop, an intriguing invitation is introduced: "Ho, every one that thirsteth, come ye to the waters, and he that hath no money; come ye, buy, and eat; yea, come, buy wine and milk without money and without price" (vs. 1). Notice that "every one" is invited. Thankfully, no one was excluded from this invitation; in fact, "The Lord is not slack concerning his promise, as some men count slackness; but is longsuffering to us-ward, not willing that *any* should perish, but that all should come to repentance" (II Peter 3:9).

> *God calls to every thirsty person, every person who realizes he is separated from God by his sin...*

God calls to every thirsty person, every person who realizes he is separated from God by his sin, inviting each one to drink the water, wine, and milk of His gracious offer without charge. The "water" symbolizes the abundance of grace and mercy available through God; the "wine" speaks of His quickening and reviving influence over a person's soul; and the "milk" denotes His ability to satisfy the longing and hunger of a wayward soul if a person will only come to Him.[16]

This invitation, clearly spelled out again in Isaiah 55:3, is unconditional: "Incline your ear, and come unto me: hear, and your soul shall live; and I will make an everlasting covenant with you, even the sure mercies of David." This offer is non-negotiable—it cannot be bought, valued, or earned. Simply, a person must hearken to His voice and come to Him on His terms. This is exactly the need of mankind. This world and all of its temporal pursuits leaves us empty and thirsty for something more. God asks this question, "Wherefore do ye spend money for that which is not bread? And your labour for that which satisfieth not? Hearken diligently unto me, and eat ye that which is good, and let your soul delight itself in fatness" (Isaiah 55:2). The deep thirst within our life is our soul's longing for reconciliation with its Maker. This intriguing invitation provides an opportunity for us to come to God and have this deep need of our souls satisfied.

An Inventive Solution

But how is this remedy to be made available? Wonderfully, the Solution, the Lord Jesus Christ, is introduced in Isaiah 55:4-5: "Behold, I have given him for a witness to the people, a leader and commander to the people. Behold, thou shalt call a nation that thou knowest not, and nations that knew not thee shall run unto thee because of the LORD thy God, and for the Holy One of Israel; for he hath glorified thee."

There has never been greater words written than those expressed in John 3:16: "For God so loved the world that He gave His only begotten Son; that whosoever believeth in Him should not perish, but have everlasting life." Mankind was hopelessly separated from God because of sin, but God in His mercy sought to reconcile man unto Himself. This was done by introducing His Son, Jesus Christ the Messiah, into the world.

> *Jesus came into this world with the purpose of dying in our place; that we, through His death, might be made alive in Him.*

Jesus came into this world with the purpose of dying in our place; that we, through His death, might be made alive in Him. "So Christ was once offered to bear the sins of many; and unto them that look for Him shall He appear the second time without sin unto salvation" (Hebrews 9:28). Our inherited sin nature from Adam has condemned us to death, but through Christ's payment for our sin on the cross we can be delivered from this bondage of death and reunited with God. I Corinthians 15:22 expresses this truth: "For as in Adam all die, even so in Christ shall all be made alive."

An Implied Limitation

Certainly at this point, there should be no doubt in your mind that you must come to Christ if you are to have eternal life in Heaven. The Scripture clearly communicates the futility of trying to earn your way to Heaven. Further, the Bible clearly identifies Christ as the only Solution for escape from the awful penalty of your sin, which is separation from God in Hell forever. However, a dangerous possibility is alluded to in this verse, "Seek ye the Lord while He may be found; call ye upon Him while He is near" (Isaiah 55:6). His gracious invitation to you is only limited in its scope by the decision of your heart.

> *His gracious invitation to you is only limited in its scope by the decision of your heart.*

Perhaps you have realized the things mentioned above are true and intend to accept Christ's invitation as your Solution for eternal life; yet you have put this decision off, planning to settle your account with God somewhere down the road. In fact, at this point you may be about to go on to the next chapter, or perhaps set this book aside. Before you do, may I ask you a question? How could something in this temporal life cause you to neglect the most important plan of all, your plan for eternity? Sadly, many people have delayed their acceptance of Christ, but have never had another opportunity to act upon their intention to alter their eternal destination. May I present a case in opposition to your delay?

First of all, don't take for granted the working of God in your life. The Scripture plainly teaches that God's Spirit will not always strive with man (Genesis 6:3). Just because God is dealing with you today does not mean that God will continue to deal with you in the future, bringing you to a place of repentance and faith in Him.

The second thing you must consider is the brevity of life. James 4:14 says, "Whereas, ye know not what shall be on the morrow. For what is your life? It is even a vapour that appeareth for a little while and then vanisheth away." Consider the wisdom of Proverbs 27:1, "Boast not thyself of tomorrow; for thou knowest not what a day may bring forth." Reality is, you are not guaranteed another moment on this earth. Death is a certain appointment whose time is only known by God. Hopefully, it will be later rather than sooner, but you should not gamble your eternal destination based on an assumption of more time on this earth.

Thirdly, you must consider the reality that life draws us further and further away from God, rather than bringing us closer to God. The reason for this, once again, is because of sin. Remember the illustration of the leaf? The Scripture teaches, "Our iniquities, like the wind, have taken us away" (Isaiah 64:6c). Just as a dead leaf is blown farther and farther away from the tree, the older you get the farther away you will get from God and the less likely you will be to consider the issue of eternal life.

Fourthly, and most important of all, you must consider the reality that there is a real enemy of God who is resisting your coming to the knowledge of the truth. This enemy's name is Satan. II Corinthians 4:3-4 says, "But if our gospel be hid, it is hid to them that are lost: in whom the god of this world [Satan] hath blinded the minds of them which believe not, lest the light of the glorious gospel of Christ, who is the image of God, should shine unto them." Friend, it is no accident that you are reading this appeal to your soul. Satan has wanted to keep you from embracing the truth all your life. As soon as you lay this book down, he will again start to work in your heart to keep you from coming to the light of the glorious gospel of Christ. Satan, who has long been the enemy of God, desires to keep everyone blinded and alienated from the truth of what is found in Jesus Christ. Satan does not want you to spend eternity in Heaven; rather, he would like for you to spend eternity suffering in Hell, which has been promised as his eternal destination.

> *There is repentance demanded as a condition of your acceptance of His gracious invitation.*

It is vital that you pay attention to this invitation God is giving to you and respond by deciding for Christ.

An Imploring Demand

"Let the wicked forsake his way, and the unrighteous man his thoughts: and let him return unto the LORD" (Isaiah 55:7). This demand to return to Jehovah God can only be met through the atoning work of His Son, the Lord Jesus Christ. Acts 4:12 reminds us, "Neither is there salvation in any other: for there is none other name under heaven given among men, whereby we must be saved." This imploring demand requires you to come to Christ. This involves a decision of your will.

There is repentance demanded as a condition of your acceptance of His gracious invitation. This repentance is a work of the Holy Spirit that brings you to a place of being willing to acknowledge the truth (II Timothy 2:25). Jesus said, "The time is fulfilled, and the kingdom of God is at hand: repent ye, and believe the gospel" (Mark 1:15). This type of repentance gets serious about dealing with sin, not on your terms, but on God's terms. You must be convinced there is nothing you can do to save yourself; but, at the same time, be thirsty for the water, wine, and milk of His offer (Isaiah 55:1)—knowing that Christ is your only hope. You must agree with God and embrace the reality of Titus 3:5: "Not by works of righteousness which we have done, but according to his mercy he saved us, by the washing of regeneration, and renewing of the Holy Ghost."

This imploring demand to forsake sin and come to God can only be met by a conscious decision on your part to accept the Lord Jesus Christ as your personal Saviour. You must ask God to forgive your sin, placing your faith and trust in Jesus Christ's finished work on the cross to pay your sin penalty. You simply accept the gift of eternal life through the work that Jesus Christ has already done on the cross—giving up on any effort within yourself to merit eternal life. What a wonderful promise: "For whosoever shall call upon the name of the Lord shall be saved" (Romans 10:13).

Friend, you now have a choice to make. The Bible makes it clear: "He that believeth on Him is not condemned; but he that believeth not is condemned already" (John 3:18). Jesus Christ is willing and able to forgive you of your sin and guarantee you a place in Heaven. What would you like to do with this demand? He makes an invitation personally to you. Revelation 3:20 says, "Behold, I stand at the door and knock. If any man hear my voice and open the door I will come in to him, and will sup with him and he with me." Won't you take Christ at His word and pray this prayer, meaning it from your heart?

> Dear God, I know that I am a sinner and because of sin, I am separated from you. I believe your Son, Jesus, died on the cross to pay for all my sin. The best I know how, I ask forgiveness for my sin and choose to rely on Jesus, by faith, to take me to Heaven when I die. Thank you for this assurance of Heaven. Amen.

An Irrevocable Guarantee

After the imploring demand, notice the irrevocable guarantee found in the rest of the verse, "Let the wicked forsake his way, and the unrighteous man his thoughts: and let him return unto the LORD, and he will have mercy upon him; and to our God, for he will abundantly pardon" (Isaiah 55:7). If you have just prayed the above prayer, you can rest assured that God has abundantly forgiven your sin, accepting Christ's payment by His sacrificial death on Calvary. "And Jesus said unto them, I am the bread of life: he that cometh to me shall never hunger; and he that believeth on me shall never thirst. [. . .] All that the Father giveth me shall come to me; and him that cometh to me I will in no wise cast out" (John 6:35 and 37). What a wonderful guarantee!

There are several things that should be pointed out about this guarantee. First of all, the pardon is complete. Notice the words "abundantly pardon" in Isaiah 55:7. It is wonderful to know that all of your sin—past, present, and future—is forgiven and placed under the blood of the Lord Jesus Christ. "As far as the east is from the west, so far hath he removed our transgressions from us" (Psalms 103:12). Your eternity is settled because of your faith and trust in what He has already done, not in what you are going to do in the future.

Secondly, there is another thought, which ought to be expounded. This concerns God's reasoning for forgiving us as He does. This explanation is given in Isaiah 55:8-11, "For my thoughts are not your thoughts, neither are your ways my ways, saith the LORD. For as the heavens are higher than the earth, so are my ways higher than your ways, and my thoughts than your thoughts. For as the rain cometh down, and the snow from heaven, and returneth not thither, but watereth the earth, and maketh it bring forth and bud, that it may give seed to the sower, and bread to the eater: so shall my word be that goeth forth out of my mouth: it shall not return unto me void, but it shall accomplish that which I please, and it shall prosper in the thing whereto I sent it."

We really cannot adequately understand why God would forgive sinners, but we rejoice in His wonderful plan that forgives and abundantly pardons. If you have made this decision for Christ, you can rest assured based on His promise and guarantee that you have been "passed from death unto life," never to return to the sentence of death. Jesus said, "Verily, verily, I say unto you, He that heareth my word, and believeth on him that sent me, hath everlasting life, and shall not come into condemnation; but is passed from death unto life" (John 5:24).

In Conclusion

"For ye shall go out with joy, and be led forth with peace: the mountains and the hills shall break forth before you into singing, and all the trees of the field shall clap their hands. Instead of the thorn shall come up the fir tree, and instead of the brier shall come up the myrtle tree: and it shall be to the LORD for a name, for an everlasting sign that shall not be cut off" (Isaiah 55:12-13). Life has new meaning when you have an eternal perspective. What a joy to realize that this life is not all there is and real meaning is found when you begin a relationship with God. Remember King Solomon? Notice his counsel, "Let us hear the conclusion of the whole matter: Fear God, and keep his commandments: for this is the whole duty of man" (Ecclesiastes 12:13).

At the close of this mortal life, eternal life will be just beginning. Have you settled the most important plan of all? If so, what a wonderful thought to know that Heaven is your eternal home because of God's marvelous mercy.

PART THREE

Process of Execution

CHAPTER ELEVEN

Putting Things in Motion

The steward's plan seemed to be exactly what he needed to salvage his faltering career. It had all the potential in the world, but would not have benefited him in the least unless he could translate a mere idea into effective action—he had to execute the plan! You can imagine how his heart must have been pounding... He could see his opportunity, but he knew that pulling off this whole scheme could be risky. His mind whirled with indecision... "Perhaps I should just walk away and hope for the best... But, what about my career? What will people think? What if I'm on the street? Maybe I should just wait... Certainly the boss and I can work things out."

Somehow he found the courage to do what deep in his heart he knew he had to do, "So he called every one of his lord's debtors unto him [. . .]" (Luke 16:5). It was deliberate action on his part that brought his subversive plan from the drawing board to the drama stage playing out his rescue from disaster.

In Exodus 14, the story is told of the Israelites fleeing before the Egyptians only to come face to face with the Red Sea, hemmed in on each side by the wilderness. With fear gripping their hearts, they prayed to God, loudly accusing Moses of leading them into the wilderness to die. Moses courageously spoke on God's behalf, "Fear ye not, stand still, and see the salvation of the LORD, which he will shew to you today: for the Egyptians whom ye have seen today, ye shall see them again no more for ever. The LORD shall fight for you, and ye shall hold your peace" (Exodus 14:13-14). He then prayed to God and God responded, "Wherefore criest thou unto me? Speak unto the children of Israel, that they go forward" (Exodus 14:15).

God told Moses it was time to quit praying and start performing! It was as if God was saying, "Get over your fear and go forward by faith." The planning and preparation had taken place. Now, with the Egyptian army hot on their trail, it was time to get busy. Moses got up on his feet, with the plan of God in his heart, and led the people victoriously across the Red Sea. God gave complete victory over the Egyptian army because the children of Israel were willing to put His plan in motion.

> *At some point in our planning and preparation, we must decide that we have a workable plan and then begin by putting things in motion.*

Along these lines, remember the admonishment found in James? "But be ye doers of the word, and not hearers only, deceiving your own selves. [. . .] But whoso looketh into the perfect law of liberty, and continueth therein, he being not a forgetful hearer, but a doer of the work, this man shall be blessed in his deed" (James 1:22&25). In this passage a blessing is promised for actually *doing* what is right; whereas, several chapters later there is a warning issued, "Therefore to him that knoweth to do good, and doeth it not, to him it is sin" (James 4:17). At some point in our planning and preparation, we must decide that we have a workable plan and then begin by putting things in motion. This is what James was emphasizing: all of our planning is completely meaningless unless deliberate action is taken to bring the plan to life.

Perhaps some hesitate at this point because of a fear of failure. It is true that executing a well-laid-out plan does not mean that you will be successful, but by putting things into motion you are able to rule out things that do not work and know better how to restructure your plan in order to try again.

Others may feel overwhelmed and wonder what good it would be to even try. You may realize the odds are small of making a sizable contribution while working your plan. There might even be a tendency to give up in despair—even before you've given it your best shot. Many things seem overwhelming, but nothing is going to ever change until we start doing something! Maybe you won't accomplish everything you have envisioned, but at least you will be making progress.

I remember ministering to a terminally ill patient. At the start of the illness the patient had been optimistic about recovery and determined to fight the disease but, as the months wore on and strength weakened, determination changed to despondency. Before one of my visits to the hospital, the family told me that the patient had quit eating and was depressed to the point of wanting to die. The doctors had prescribed a routine of treatment that promised a ray of hope but, in the patient's weakened condition, they had been unable to proceed. If the patient would eat, maybe the treatments could progress. When I got to the hospital, I took the patient by the hand and said, "I know that you are discouraged and things don't look too good, but you have got to get back in the fight." We went on to discuss the circumstances and then I wrapped up the conversation with this admonishment, "If you get back in the fight I can't guarantee you a win; but if you don't get back in the fight I can guarantee you a loss. At least, if you give it your best shot, you will know that you did all you could."

If God has given you a plan to help achieve His goal, then you have His divine help to see the goal accomplished. He must bring the plan into reality, but He has chosen to work through human instruments in accomplishing His will. Cooperate with Him by courageously taking a step of faith and putting things in motion.

~ ~ ~

Opening day has finally rolled around. The grueling preparation of spring training is a shadow in your memory as you swing the bat in the on-deck circle. Pine rosin, leather, and the smell of freshly cut grass fills your nostrils, as the smooth feel of wood feels cold and lifeless in your hands. You hear thousands of fans chanting your name, who eagerly wait for you to connect with the ball. The television cameras stare in silence reminding you of millions of people across the world sitting glued to the set, watching your every move. A glance over to the dugout picks up the signal from the coach as your name is announced over the loud speaker. A cold sweat emerges on your brow as you step up to home plate. Nervously, you adjust your helmet as you look out over the manicured field dotted with uniformed players that crouch in readiness. The catcher gives the signal and the pitcher winds up to throw. The crowd is screaming, "Hey, batter batter; hey, batter batter. . ." The ball is released. It's heading straight down the middle. . . A swing of your bat could bring the field alive with action. You hear the crowd yell, "Swing!"

~ ~ ~

Will you swing the bat?

CHAPTER TWELVE

Developing Your Team

A great rifle shot off the end of your bat into right field will only get you to first base. It will be up to your team to get you around the bases and home. Maybe you will hit the ball out of the ballpark, but winning the game will rely on the rest of the team doing their part both offensively and defensively. No games are won with just an all-star player.

You will only be as good as the people you surround yourself with—and by all means surround yourself with people. Working in concert with others can accomplish so much more for the cause of Christ. Moses seemed to imply, in Deuteronomy 32:30, that two people working together could increase their effectiveness ten-fold! What then could a *team* of workers do? The accomplishments of a number of people working toward the same goal are staggering, proven many times over in the realm of business. You have got to have a team, an inner-circle of people around you that you can trust!

Moses learned this valuable lesson of teamwork early while leading the Israelites out of bondage in Egypt. Numbers 11 relates the story to us:

> 11 And Moses said unto the LORD, Wherefore hast thou afflicted thy servant? And wherefore have I not found favour in thy sight, that thou layest the burden of all this people upon me?
>
> 12 Have I conceived all this people? Have I begotten them, that thou shouldest say unto me, Carry them in thy bosom, as a nursing father beareth the sucking child, unto the land which thou swarest unto their fathers?
>
> 13 Whence should I have flesh to give unto all this people? For they weep unto me, saying, Give us flesh, that we may eat.
>
> 14 I am not able to bear all this people alone, because it is too heavy for me.
>
> 15 And if thou deal thus with me, kill me, I pray thee, out of hand, if I have found favour in thy sight; and let me not see my wretchedness.
>
> 16 And the LORD said unto Moses, Gather unto me seventy men of the elders of Israel, whom thou knowest to be the elders of the people, and officers over them; and bring them unto the tabernacle of the congregation, that they may stand there with thee.
>
> 17 And I will come down and talk with thee there: and I will take of the spirit which is upon thee, and will put it upon them; and they shall bear the burden of the people with thee, that thou bear it not thyself alone.

Moses was almost defeated and ready to give up until he realized that he must develop a team of capable people around him to help share the load. There are several things about developing a team which can be gleaned from this account.

Communication

First of all, before you put anyone on your team, remember that up-front communication sets the atmosphere for the rest of the working relationship. Find out who this person is and what their track record is before asking him or her to join the team. Notice what the Lord said unto Moses,

"Gather unto me seventy men of the elders of Israel, whom *thou knowest to be the elders of the people*" (Exodus 11:16a). The choice of Moses' team should be influenced by what he knew about their character and reputation.

One of our modern conveniences is the availability of whipped topping. It has replaced the chore of making real whipped cream. It looks and tastes similar to whipped cream, but anyone who has had the real thing will tell you that in comparison, whipped topping is really "artificial fluff." As you review possible candidates, you will find a lot of folks who are nothing but "artificial fluff." They look genuine at first glance, but they are not what they appear to be. As a leader, you must be diligent enough to do your "homework" enabling you to discern who is genuine.

Further, explain to prospective team members your expectations, making certain there is no doubt in their mind what will be expected of them if they are invited and agree to join the effort. The reason for Moses recruiting these men is obvious: "[. . .] bring them unto the tabernacle of the congregation, that they may *stand there with thee*" (Exodus 11:16c). These men would be working in close harmony with Moses, day in, and day out. Likewise, the team you recruit will share in your ministry and you want to be certain they understand the part they will be asked to perform. If they are unhappy about your expectations, a good time to find that out is *before* asking them to join the team. Also, be sure they are willing to work within your structure and be loyal to your leadership. These things should top the list of your discussion for they are vital to successful working relationships.

Along these lines, it is a good idea to discuss upfront the possibility that things may not work out. Be careful of making long-term commitments to people who join your team. Explain that positions within your team are maintained by performance. If they are asked to join the effort, it will be on a trial basis at first to see how things work out. During the first several months, they may decide they are not comfortable being on the team or you may decide they are not what you really need. Either way, leave your options open as long as possible.

Qualification

Secondly, get the best-qualified people available on your team. The Lord instructed Moses, not only to select men whom he knew to be reputable, but also men who were "officers over them," or men who had leadership ability and were already respected among their peers as such. Likewise, don't be afraid of the success of potential team members. Seek qualified, respectable people who have a burden for the plan the Lord has given you. Then, harness their ability and put it to work accomplishing the objectives you feel the Lord has laid on your heart. As a leader, you do not have to possess all the skills necessary to accomplish the goal; however, if the goal is to be accomplished you must find capable people who share your vision and will come alongside you, joining in the effort under your leadership.

Reproduction

Thirdly, while developing your team, seek to reproduce yourself in the people you surround yourself with. The Lord told Moses, "[. . .] I will take of the spirit which is upon thee, and will put it upon them [. . .]" (Exodus 11:17b). II Timothy 2:2 instructs us, "And the things that thou hast heard of me among many witnesses, the same commit thou to faithful men, who shall be able to teach others also." As a leader, it is your responsibility to teach your followers the things God has taught you. Help them understand the goals and plans you believe He would have the team to carry out. With the fast pace and duties of leadership, don't overlook the important step of reproduction.

> *Don't be afraid of the success of potential team members.*

It is said of James Boswell, the famous biographer of Samuel Johnson, that he often referred to a special day in his childhood when his father took him fishing. The day was fixed in his adult mind, and he often reflected upon many of the things his father had taught him in the course of their fishing experience together. After having heard of that particular excursion so often, it occurred to someone much later to check the journal that Boswell's father kept and determine what had been said about the fishing trip from the parental perspective. Turning to that date, the reader found only one sentence entered: "Gone fishing today with my son—a day wasted."[17]

Little did Mr. Boswell know. . . That "day wasted" would be a turning point in the molding of a man who would one day greatly impact the world of classical literature. We must remind ourselves that time spent reproducing ourselves is never wasted, but invested. Your team will be richly rewarded with enhanced performance and efficiency. Further, the

Lord may lead you or someone on your team to another place of service somewhere down the road. What you've reproduced in them will help shape their future, allowing them to be used by the Lord in a greater way. One last thought; although it is your responsibility to teach your followers, you will find they will teach you a great deal if you are willing to listen to them. Treat them with respect and be open to the input they give from their perspective.

Function

Lastly, give your team members responsibility over an area and allow them room to function. The Lord instructed Moses to delegate some of his burden to the leaders he had chosen: "[. . .] they shall bear the burden of the people with thee, that thou bear it not thyself alone" (Exodus 11:17c). If you have to be involved in every decision, why have a team in the first place? Pledge your support to the people who work under you and let them know you have confidence in them. Assure them they will never have to guess where you stand: if you feel they are wrong, you will tell them where they are wrong—privately, if possible; if they are right and do a good job, they can expect to be rewarded, both privately and openly.

In Conclusion

Many times in the realm of the Lord's work, we depend on volunteers. You may feel there is no one available to help, but you will be amazed at the people who will participate if they are asked. One of the greatest hindrances to getting volunteers to help is a lack of organization and planning. To secure help you must know where you are going, and be able to communicate to others how they can get involved, helping you accomplish a worthwhile work.

It has been discussed how to develop a team, but what if you inherit a team that someone else has built? Many times it is a great blessing, but just as often it is a huge hassle. The difference depends on the team's adaptability to you as their new leader. No two people are going to do things exactly the same way and people are slow to change. Over the long haul, many new leaders end up finding their own people.

When you are faced with a situation where it seems inevitable you will have to rebuild the team, be patient. Eventually, people may find somewhere else to go because, chances are, they are not any happier with you being their leader than you are with them being your followers. When someone does leave, be ready with a replacement.

When people have to be replaced, do so slowly and cautiously. Try to avoid a revolution—many times new leaders find themselves caught in the crossfire and get blown off the team. Don't be afraid to "lay low" awhile. Keep your purposes and goals alive in your heart and wait until you have a chance to put them in place. Opportunity will knock . . . make sure you are there to answer the door. In the meantime, keep working to develop the team the Lord has given you.

CHAPTER THIRTEEN

Becoming a Team Player

At one time, the steward of Luke 16 seems to have been an outstanding team player but, by the time we are introduced to him in Scripture, we find a man falling apart, drowning in doubt and suspicion. With his career in jeopardy, he did show brilliant planning and execution to influence his future; nevertheless, he was clearly "unjust" by choosing to do so at the owner's expense. The actions he took to salvage his faltering career obviously did not have the best interests of the team in mind; however, it is unclear whether or not this was always the case. Perhaps the accusations made against him, putting his career in jeopardy, were the catalyst that hurled him into this destructive mode. Or, maybe he had ventured down this path of corruption long before, just as his accusers said. We do not know for sure, because we are not told the outcome of the owner's investigation.

If his accusers told the truth, then their actions were justifiable, motivated by concern for the team. If his accusers lied, they sacrificed not only the steward's reputation to advance their selfish interests, but also the stability and welfare of the team. Regardless of where blame is placed, clearly teamwork was cast aside and everyone suffered as a result of self-centeredness.

Becoming a team player does not happen overnight; in fact, the concept of teamwork is something that must be developed in each of us. Our greatest strength is found when working with others who share a common goal; yet it seems the most difficult thing we do is join with others in a concerted effort. Ephesians 4:15-16 explains that teamwork is a step of growth toward maturity in Christ: "But speaking the truth in love, may grow up into him in all things, which is the head, even Christ: from whom the whole body fitly joined together and compacted by that which every joint supplieth, according to the effectual working in the measure of every part, maketh increase of the body unto the edifying of itself in love." The scope of this verse encompasses the Church, all the saved who make up the body of Christ. This verse explains that when the Church is working together—each one fulfilling their responsibility toward accomplishing the goal of increasing and building up the body—there are effective, healthy results.

In the previous chapter, our thoughts were primarily directed to the role of the leader in developing his team. In this chapter we will focus on both the leader and the follower's role of becoming a team player. In using the terminology, "team player," we will consider the believer's responsibility to the body of Christ as a whole, but more specifically to the local church or ministry, with which each believer is affiliated. Turning to Hebrews 12:1-4, we find ten positive truths that motivate us concerning this responsibility:

> 1 Wherefore seeing we also are compassed about with so great a cloud of witnesses, let us lay aside every weight, and the sin which doth so easily beset us, and let us run with patience the race that is set before us,
>
> 2 Looking unto Jesus the author and finisher of our faith; who for the joy that was set before him endured the cross, despising the shame, and is set down at the right hand of the throne of God.
>
> 3 For consider him that endured such contradiction of sinners against himself, lest ye be wearied and faint in your minds.
>
> 4 Ye have not yet resisted unto blood, striving against sin.

Positive Peers

Notice verse one, "Wherefore seeing we also are compassed about with so great a cloud of witnesses [. . .]." Think about the great heroes of the faith found in Hebrews 11 that this verse is referring to: men and women like Abraham, Sara, Jacob, Moses, Joshua, and Rahab. These, and many others like them, cooperated with God's plan, working alongside others to accomplish His will. At the time of their death each left unfinished work, trusting members of the team to carry it forth. These peers from the past should motivate and encourage us to join in their efforts to further the kingdom of God.

Not only are there positive peers from the past, but think of those around you who are cheering you on, impacted by the contributions you make to the efforts of Christ. Think of the ones who were responsible for you coming to know Christ as your Saviour and those who have helped in your discipleship. Think of the people in your local church, your family, and other Christian friends who are serving the Lord around the world. These peers are all a part of a team that surrounds you and they are counting on you to make your life count for Christ.

There could be no greater motivation to be a team player than realizing the encouragement that comes through working with others who share your burden. There are thousands of voices all around us and echoing down the hallways of history who are a testimony for us if we become a team player; however, our life is a testament against them if we fail to join with others in this great work.

Positive Passion

Because we have these positive peers counting on us, we are admonished to "lay aside every weight" (Hebrews 12:1). To become a team player, you must adopt the passion of the team. This passion becomes so strong that everything else is secondary in importance to its being fulfilled. The Apostle Paul captured the passion of the team, "But what things were gain to me, those I counted loss for Christ. Yea doubtless, and I count all things but loss for the excellency of the knowledge of Christ Jesus my Lord: for whom I have suffered the loss of all things, and do count them but dung, that I may win Christ" (Philippians 3:7-8).

So many believers are hindered from embracing this positive passion. Paul wrote the church at Galatia, "Ye did run well; who did hinder you that ye should not obey the truth?" (Galatians 5:7). Maybe you started out working for the cause of Christ, but something has taken the place of this passion. The team is calling for you to re-order your priorities, laying "aside every weight" to be once again effective in carrying out this positive passion!

Positive Performance

Hebrews 12:1 continues, "[. . .] let us lay aside every weight, and the sin which doth so easily beset us [. . .]." Along with the responsibility of working with peers to fulfill a shared passion comes the benefit of accountability. The more you realize others on the team are counting on you, the more motivation you will have to do the right things in the sight of God. Sin against God is detrimental, not only to yourself, but also to everyone on the team who is seeking to do a work for God. Do you remember the warning in James? "Then when lust hath conceived, it bringeth forth sin: and sin, when it is finished, bringeth forth death. Do not err, my beloved brethren" (James 1:15-16).

The enemy delights in keeping believers from a positive performance. When out of fellowship with the team and trying to serve the Lord all alone, a believer is vulnerable to the temptation of Satan. A great antidote to this is joining with a group of people who are seeking to please God with their lives. Then, get busy in that group trying to make a difference for the cause of Christ.

Positive Pressure

Notice the last part of Hebrews 12:1, "[. . .] and let us run with patience the race that is set before us." Borrowing an analogy from the realm of athletics, this passage encourages us to "run [. . .] the race." When you join the efforts of a team, you inherit its burden, creating positive pressure in your soul to accomplish the work God would have you do.

Although Ephesians 2:8-9 states that we are not saved by our good works, but by God's grace; the next verse clearly explains God's purpose in giving us the gift of salvation: "For we are his [God's] workmanship, created in Christ Jesus unto good works, which God hath before ordained that we should walk in them" (Ephesians 2:10). The church at Colosse was instructed to "[. . .] walk worthy of the Lord unto all pleasing, being fruitful in every good work [. . .]" (Colossians 1:10). After admonishing the church at Philippi to work for the Lord, they are reminded: "For it is God which worketh in you both to will and to do of his good pleasure" (Philippians 2:13).

Throughout Scripture, God makes it clear that believers have been enabled by the Holy Spirit to work for the Lord, and are expected to help further His kingdom. Pressure from the team to "run" for the Lord is a positive reinforcement of the Holy Spirit's work in us.

In Matthew 20 Jesus told the story of a man hiring laborers to work in his vineyard. He goes early in the morning, probably about 6:00, to the marketplace and hires everyone he can find. He goes again at 9:00am, 12:00n, and 3:00pm. Each time he finds other laborers standing around idle, so he hires them and sends them to work. Going back to the marketplace about 5:00 in the evening he finds yet others who are standing idle and he poses this question to them, "Why stand ye here all the day idle?" Notice their answer, "Because no man hath hired us." This story illustrates a great truth: you will not accomplish much for the Lord until you feel the pressure of being on the team. The laborers were idle and unproductive until the owner of the vineyard put them to work.

Maybe you have not wanted to be "tied down" to some ministry on a regular basis—you have not been interested in this "positive pressure." Why not become a team player? The race is before us, there is a mission to fulfill. The cause of Christ pleads for you to make a difference. "By much slothfulness the building decayeth; and through idleness of the hands the house droppeth through" (Ecclesiastes 10:18).

Positive Patience

Further, we are instructed to run the race, "with patience." This pressure within our souls to accomplish the work of God must be coupled with a strong faith and confidence in the Lord's timing. This brings about steadiness and consistency in our efforts as a team player, keeping us from frustration and discouragement when results do not surface as quickly as we feel they should.

On the other hand, some have used this concept of patience as an excuse for their lack of commitment to the mission; consequently, anyone passionate about serving Christ becomes a threat to their comfort zone. In one of the Old Testament's most well known stories, David and Goliath, there is an example of such critical hypocrisy. As a soldier in the

Israeli army under King Saul, Eliab, David's oldest brother, had gone forth to battle against the Philistines. Encamped on the side of a mountain, across the valley from the Philistines, Eliab and all the hosts of Israel "were dismayed and sore afraid" (I Samuel 17:11), after hearing the challenge of Philistia's champion, Goliath. David shows up soon after this challenge is issued, having been sent by his father, and finds everyone in Israel's army, including his oldest brother, Eliab, afraid to stand up for God. Notice the exchange in I Samuel 17:26-29:

> And David spake to the men that stood by him, saying, What shall be done to the man that killeth this Philistine, and taketh away the reproach from Israel? For who is this uncircumcised Philistine, that he should defy the armies of the living God? And the people answered him after this manner, saying, So shall it be done to the man that killeth him. And Eliab his eldest brother heard when he spake unto the men; and Eliab's anger was kindled against David, and he said, Why camest thou down hither? And with whom hast thou left those few sheep in the wilderness? I know thy pride, and the naughtiness of thine heart; for thou art come down that thou mightest see the battle. And David said, What have I now done? Is there not a cause?

Being embarrassed because of David's willingness to face Goliath, Eliab brazenly accused David of three things: You are irresponsible, full of pride, and way out of line; or in modern language, "David, you are moving way too fast—you are getting ahead of the Lord's will."

However, we know that David wasn't irresponsible, God was promoting and advancing him; he did not have the wrong motives, he was motivated by passion for his Lord; and he certainly wasn't out of step with God's will, he was completely willing to sacrifice his life to protect the cause of His God. David responded to Eliab in effect, . . . I am not what you say I am, but what you or anyone else may think about me is not the most important thing. I am not after position, popularity, pomp, or prestige and you are not going to discourage or detour me. If my actions expose your uncommitted heart, then so be it, for I realize that there is more than just a social club meeting going on. . . "What have I now done? Is there not a cause?"

To translate "with patience" as "with procrastination" misconstrues the interpretation of this modifying adverbial clause of the verb "run." "With patience" is translated from the Greek words, "dia hupomone." "Dia" is a primary preposition denoting the channel of an act,[18] and "hupomone" means to have a cheerful (or hopeful) endurance, or constancy.[19] Used within this sentence, we conclude that running the race, "with patience," instructs us to channel our service to the Lord through the filter of a cheerful, hopeful endurance.

Serving the Lord is to be equated with running a marathon rather than a sprint race. Therefore, this instruction does not mean we should slow to a crawl in our service for the Lord; on the contrary, we are to "run the race," trusting the results to Him. Galatians 6:9, "And let us not be weary in well doing: for in due season we shall reap, if we faint not."

Positive Participant

Before moving on to Hebrews 12:2, there is one more positive truth to uncover in verse 1, "[. . .] and let us run with patience the race that is set before us." The race is "set before us," encompassing everyone on the Lord's team. Collectively, we have all been assigned the responsibility of serving the Lord; however, when you accept individual responsibility for a certain portion of this collective undertaking, and perform this task to the best of your ability, you uncover a real secret of staying on the team.

Notice this truth "positive participant" is singular; whereas the first truth we studied, "positive peers," was plural. Remembering there are positive peers sharing in the work of the Lord will be a great source of encouragement to you, as long as you leave your expectations for them in the Lord's hands, and stay focused on your participation in the area of work the Lord has entrusted to your care. If you are not careful, you may become discouraged with the lack of performance of others whom you feel should be doing a better job for the Lord. Stay focused on what the Lord has asked you to do and find encouragement when you know that your labor is pleasing to Him.

The Apostle Paul must have understood this concept. Notice how many times he refers to his "race" in the following three verses: "For *I* am now ready to be offered, and the time of *my* departure is at hand. *I* have fought a good fight, *I* have finished my course, *I* have kept the faith: henceforth there is laid up for *me* a crown of righteousness, which the Lord, the righteous judge, shall give *me* at that day: and not to me only, but unto all them also that love his appearing" (2 Timothy 4:6-8). Many of Paul's team members turned aside from following Christ, but he never quit the team. He knew that the Lord was keeping record and would reward him for being faithful to his calling.

You can only be responsible for what you do—for the race you run. You are not competing with your peers, but cooperating with them in a team effort. When they succeed you rejoice; when they fail you help them up, if possible, and continue on running your race.

Positive Purpose

What a purpose statement: "Looking unto Jesus the author and finisher of our faith who for the joy that was set before him endured the cross, despising the shame, and is set down at the right hand of the throne of God" (Hebrews 12:2). Just as a runner in a marathon keeps a mental image of the finish line prominently in mind, we focus on Jesus, knowing that our mission will one day be complete in Him.

II Corinthians 4:5 says, "For we preach not ourselves, but Christ Jesus the Lord; and ourselves your servants for Jesus' sake." Becoming a team player for any other purpose than herein stated will result in disappointment and defeat.

Positive Program

Notice why Jesus endured the cross, despising the shame: "for the joy that was set before him." There was no pleasure in Jesus' experience of the cross. In fact He prayed, "O my Father, if it be possible, let this cup pass from me: nevertheless not as I will, but as thou wilt" (Matthew 26:39). Jesus endured the agony of the cross because of the benefits of what was beyond.

Our vision is limited to the past and the present circumstances of our lives. We are not able to see beyond this moment in life, but we have been promised that God will make our efforts on His team worthwhile. What a tremendous promise found in Hebrews 6:10, "For God is not unrighteous to forget your work and labour of love, which ye have shewed toward his name, in that ye have ministered to the saints, and do minister." Countless other passages remind us of the joy ahead for us—both in this life and in eternity to come.

Some team members grow discouraged because they feel their work is going unnoticed; they don't feel appreciated by the team. This positive program reminds us that this is not all there is. We must choose to either focus on the journey or the destination; the trial or the triumph; the work or the reward; the weariness or the promised rest. Look beyond today with optimism for the future.

Positive Person

"For consider him that endured such contradiction of sinners against himself, lest ye be wearied and faint in your minds" (Hebrews 12:3). Pilate examined Jesus and publicly exclaimed, "I find in him no fault at all" (John 18:38). Again, Pilate affirmed, "Behold, I bring him forth to you, that ye may know that I find no fault in him" (John 19:4); yet the crowd still cried, "crucify him, crucify him" (John 19:6).

You won't be on the team long before you realize that team members are not always the positive peers they should be—in fact they do not always treat other players fairly. At these times you must determine to stay on the team, choosing to remember that you are working for a positive Person, the Lord Jesus Christ. "For what glory is it, if, when ye be buffeted for your faults, ye shall take it patiently? But if, when ye do well, and suffer for it, ye take it patiently, this is acceptable with God. For even hereunto were ye called: because Christ also suffered for us, leaving us an example, that ye should follow his steps" (I Peter 2:20-21).

Don't get so wrapped up, anticipating the positive program of the future, that you forget the importance of tending to the present. There is no greater motivation for staying faithful than realizing the extent of what the Captain of our salvation endured, that He might give us membership on the team and entrust us with this mission.

Positive Platform

The Scripture reminds us that Jesus' example of perseverance is unequalled in any of our experiences, "Ye have not yet resisted unto blood, striving against sin" (Hebrews 12:4). We have not been called upon to make the ultimate sacrifice, we haven't given our lives in His service. How can we complain or justify dropping out of the race?

You may not feel that you have as much to offer God as someone else, but you do have your life. This can be a positive platform used to further His cause. He gave His life for you, can't you give your life, becoming a team player that His message may go forth in power? "Finally, my brethren, be strong in the Lord, and in the power of his might. Put on the whole armour of God, that ye may be able to stand against the wiles of the devil" (Ephesians 6:10-11).

In Conclusion

These ten reasons all point to evidence that participating in a team effort is overwhelmingly positive! Sure, there are hurdles to overcome – some of these have been pointed out above, but our Lord designed the greatest concept in the world, the local church team. Within this structure, and supplemental to this are other ministry teams that God has brought into existence to further His kingdom. Make a strong commitment to the team where God has placed you, "Submitting yourselves one to another in the fear of God" (Ephesians 5:21).

~ ~ ~

Become a team player today!

CHAPTER FOURTEEN

Leading Your Team

So, you have set things in motion, assembled a team, and are ready to roll up your sleeves and get to work—or are you? Before getting in too deeply, there is an important issue to consider: are you prepared for the inevitable problems that will come as you lead your team?

There are three basic reasons most problems develop within a team: a lack of communication, a lack of training, or a lack of respect for the leader. Occasionally, every team has an uncooperative person that seeks to cause disruption and we will approach solutions to that later, but realistically most people want to do a good job. Most problems within an organization can be traced back to leadership.

Knowing these areas present potential problems; get ahead by employing solutions up front. The book of Proverbs gives us wonderful wisdom in this vein of thought: "A prudent man foreseeth the evil, and hideth himself: but the simple pass on, and are punished" (Proverbs 22:3).

Solution #1

One of the best things you can do to prevent problems is have regular meetings with your team. There are so many benefits: it encourages good communication, promotes training, and fosters mutual respect and understanding. It is amazing that organizations try to survive without regular meetings. What a tremendous thought is given us in Scripture, "Behold, how good and how pleasant it is for brethren to dwell together in unity" (Psalm 133:1). The word "dwell" carries with it the implication of sitting down or settling in. So much can be accomplished in a productive meeting when a team of people gathers around their leader.

On the other hand, an unorganized meeting—just to mark time off the calendar—can be counter-productive. As a leader, it is your responsibility to set the agenda for the meeting and create an atmosphere of teamwork that produces solutions rather than one that creates additional problems.

Before establishing the purposes of a meeting, we need to firmly fix in our minds what the meeting is not for. It is not a platform to publicly handle problems that should be handled privately. Embarrassing a worker will not motivate them and strengthen the team—in fact, it may go a long way toward damaging the team spirit. Proverbs 18:19 gives us age-old wisdom, "A brother offended is harder to be won than a strong city: and their contentions are like the bars of a castle." If you are trying to get someone on the campaign trail of negative publicity against the team and especially you as the leader, embarrass them in front of their peers. It should be said, that as a leader, there is a time and a place that you will have to deal with issues in a meeting that may embarrass and offend someone. When this does occur, you will then be prepared to "cut your losses" and deal with the repercussions. You will know when it is necessary, but as a general rule it is best to handle problems privately.

Further, the meeting is not an open forum to tear down other departments within the organization or criticize leadership above you. There may be questions raised involving other facets of the organization. Perhaps what they are doing, or decisions they have made negatively impact the performance of your team. If so, this may surface in your meeting. As the leader you need to hear their opinion, but you should never voice your support. You have one of two choices to make. If they have a valid complaint or some issue you feel would benefit from your expertise, inform the person raising the complaint that you will address it and get back to them as soon as possible. If their complaint is not valid, or it concerns operation policy handed down from your superiors, you must support the leadership above you. Never get in a position of siding with subordinates against leadership. It will backfire, compromising the integrity of the structure. Support and loyalty go both ways. Remember, if your leader is strong, you are that much stronger. You cannot allow your meeting to deteriorate the structure.

Lastly, the meeting is not a time for fellowship and fun. There is nothing wrong with that in the proper setting, but schedule time before or afterward. When the meeting begins it should be conducted in an orderly fashion that sets a business-like atmosphere. Your team will set the tempo of their activity based on the fervency of the meeting. Give the impression that you expect things to be accomplished by setting an example of industry and hard work during the meeting.

So, what is the purpose of the meeting? First of all, it is an excellent time to evaluate your past success. Share with the team what has been accomplished. Find what has been done right and capitalize on it. Recognize individuals with outstanding results and talk to the team about everything that has been accomplished with their help. Emphasize the importance of every single contribution to the overall effort. This is a good time to give out awards or bonuses. Your team needs to hear your approval. They need to know their leader is proud of the work they are doing. They are not the perfect team, in fact, at times, it seems they should be reprimanded for what they are doing wrong, rather than bragging on what they are doing right; however, as a general rule, you will be amazed at how much more will be accomplished by bragging rather than bashing.

For instance, let's say that you are having a Sunday school teacher's meeting. One of the problems you have is getting teachers to come to their classes early on Sunday morning. You have been embarrassed when people arrive and find an empty classroom. You have asked them to come early several times and it seems they continue to slide in at the last minute. Try this approach: find a teacher who is always early. This teacher may have been coming early for years, and you can always count on him/her to be there. Have this teacher stand at the meeting and recognize him with an award or gift for his diligence and punctuality. Brag about him and publicly tell him how much it means to have him there early every Sunday. Explain how nice it is to know that his room is always staffed and ready for visitors. Have everyone give this teacher a round of applause. If you handle it right, you will be amazed at how effective it will be in motivating everyone else.

Another purpose of the meeting is to exchange ideas. Your team needs a chance to tell you what is going on and you need to keep them informed as well. They also need an opportunity to coordinate their efforts with the rest of the team. Get the ball rolling by asking a question such as, "So, how is everything going out there?" Go on to say something like this, "Ladies and Gentlemen, this is not a time to point a finger, but it is a time to lend a hand." Make it understood this is a time to seek solutions, not just complain and air all grievances. Have you ever stopped to consider that everyone in every organization has something about which they are not happy? You are not inviting a pity party, but you are looking for trouble spots that, if fixed, will help the team's effectiveness.

> *When opinions are given, you are not obligated to agree or disagree. In fact, it is generally a good idea to thank the person for his input and tell him that you will think it over.*

As a leader, you need to hear from your team. Once again, it is not your job to have all the answers. You are there together to help find solutions. Ask their advice about decisions you are making that will impact them. These are your key people who hopefully are as concerned about reaching the goal as you are. Allow them to voice their opinion and have a part in developing solutions.

When opinions are given, you are not obligated to agree or disagree. In fact, it is generally a good idea to thank the person for his input and tell him that you will think it over. You are the leader and you must make the final decision. If you disagree right away, you probably will discourage your team from making any suggestions. Before you dismiss an idea from your team, consider that they may know what they are talking about. Give it some thought! Again, you are not obligated to have an answer to all their questions. A simple, "That's a good question and I need some time to think it over" is generally a good answer.

You will hear a lot of advice and many questions will be raised in meetings that people have not really thought through. Because of this, what they have said or asked is not really important to them or to the team. It is said in the heat of the moment—more for affect than for effect. You may never need to address the comment or question. As soon as it is spoken and you respond, it will be forgotten by everyone. However, if you respond by addressing the issue instead of validating and sidestepping it, your response as the leader will not be forgotten. What was an innocent "bird flying by" may become a vulture eating away at the communication you are trying to foster. If the issue or question is more than a "fly-by" it will surface again. When and if it does, you will have had time to prepare an appropriate answer.

Meetings are also a great time to share the plan. Be careful of sharing the whole plan—as a followers they may not be able to see the whole vision. They just need a piece of it at a time. Share with your team immediate goals, breaking down the entire plan a step at a time. When you meet, review your progress and give them insight into where you are trying to go next. Divide up responsibilities and assign tasks to individuals. Doing this in a team meeting allows everyone to understand how they fit into the overall process, helps them understand the importance of the job they have been assigned, and makes them accountable.

Your success as a leader will be determined by your ability to effectively communicate your plan and inspire participation in its fulfillment. You will have to constantly review the plan with the team, keeping them focused on the goals that have been set. Remember, what seems crystal clear to you may take months for your people to truly grasp. Repetition is a key to learning—don't be afraid to constantly repeat yourself until you feel the team understands your direction and is able to contribute to the effort effectively.

Solution #2

Hand-in-hand with regular meetings, you need to have an adequate training program in place. There must be a vehicle to bring exchanged information into the realm of reality. The following paragraphs contain insight into areas you should consider as you develop a training program.

People are motivated by mentoring. With training comes confidence and cooperation in a joint effort. An experienced, loyal worker should carefully train each team member. To start with, that will be you as the leader.

Novices are not natives. Don't expect a person just starting out to perform as well as you do. You are at your level because of years of experience. What comes naturally to you will take time to become second nature to them. You must be willing to retrain over and over again. This requires having some type of ongoing training in place.

People are sometimes oblivious to what seems obvious. You can't expect people to read your mind! Nor can you expect them to look around and naturally know what needs to be done. You may have that ability—you are the leader! It isn't a lack of common sense for your team to not have the insight God has given you. That is why they have a leader. Spell out expectations of each job—in writing if possible. Don't assume people know what is expected. As you train, break their job down into simple steps, training them from start to finish—in even the obvious!

People are prone to predicaments. Pastor James Avaritt once advised me, "Expect people to be people and then you won't be surprised when people are people." Expect the best from your team, but prepare for the worst. In your training, set forth clear boundaries that will govern the working relationship. If you wait until you have a problem to create a guideline, it places too much emphasis on the ones who are in the predicament. When you can predict a problem and have a well thought out solution in place, things will go much smoother when the predicaments come—and they will come.

Unfortunately, sometimes people are quick to quit. What would you do if a trusted associate was no longer with you tomorrow morning? Could you make it? Do you have a plan to function in their absence? Like it or not, people oftentimes do not help you make a smooth transition. In all fairness, there are sometimes extenuating circumstances that cause someone to quit or be unavailable without adequate notice. Be prepared by cross-training. Make sure several people know and have access to every job. It is ideal if you as the leader know everyone's job well enough to carry out its function. Never be without a back-up plan.

People at times are reluctant to retrain. Once someone is trained incorrectly, it is hard to retrain them correctly. Make sure they are taught the right way the first time.

Lastly, people sometimes are not suitable. No matter how long you train or work with them, they just don't ever seem to grasp the job. They are not "stuck on stupid," but probably are not suitable for the job you are trying to fit them into. Because you have told them up front this is a trial run, you can easily reassign them to something else.

Solution #3

Money can buy solutions to the above-mentioned need for training and just about anyone can establish a regular meeting; however, this last solution focuses on something special—the leader. Organizations flounder when there is no respect for leadership. The following suggestions do not guarantee respect, but will heavily contribute to success if observed.

If you want to be respected, you have to be respectable. This means you will have to set the pace—you have got to work. Your followers will not be more dedicated than you are. Accept the responsibility, which comes with the privilege of being their leader, and put your shoulder to the plow.

Another truth to consider: you cannot lead people to a place where you have never been. Take time to follow the right steps to gain experience and qualifications necessary to earn the respect of the people you lead.

As the leader, you must acknowledge your followers. Give them credit where credit is due. Just as important, give them reward where reward is due—and sometimes when it is not due. If you are generous in sharing the load, be generous in sharing the wealth. Well informed, valued, and compensated workers are happy team members. When workers feel they do all the work and their leader gets all the reward, they soon lose respect and confidence in their leadership.

CHAPTER FIFTEEN

Following Your Leader

Followers are the backbone of an organization's successful execution of their plan, but are usually its unsung heroes. Society places a lot of emphasis on leadership development and leaders receive much of the reward in most organizations. This might lead someone to the unfortunate conclusion that following is somehow less important than leading, but that just isn't so. Every person has been designed and equipped by the Creator for a unique function within each team. David rejoiced in this truth: "I will praise thee; for I am fearfully and wonderfully made: marvelous are thy works; and that my soul knoweth right well." Within God's economy, there is no surplus, no misfits, and no mistakes. He places equal value upon every human being; leader or follower; however, He desires each one to function according to His design.

We have seen from Luke 16 the damage followers can inflict on an organization when they subvert leadership. In Deuteronomy chapter one, Moses gives us an up-close, nostalgic view of Israel's ignominy in this area. Instead of receiving great blessings from God, their destructive decisions brought great heartache to themselves and their leader. In their reasoning, they made five fatal mistakes: they disregarded their leader's instructions; they decided to complain and murmur; they delighted in men more than in God; they denied God's work; and finally defied God's plan. Their failure to follow leadership resulted in heavy casualties in battle, denied entry to the Promised Land, and wandering in the wilderness for forty years. From this account we glean tremendous lessons for those who seek to follow leadership God has placed over them.

Consider the Source

Coming to the brink of great blessings, Moses had commanded Israel: "Behold, the LORD thy God hath set the land before thee: go up and possess it, as the LORD God of thy fathers hath said unto thee; fear not, neither be discouraged" (Deuteronomy 1:21). Moses' command was not anything new, or bizarre to the children of Israel, neither was he acting arbitrarily. Acting in good faith and on the behalf of God, he gave orders to execute the plan God had designed.

The people responded, "We will send men before us, and they shall search us out the land, and bring us word again by what way we must go up, and into what cities we shall come" (Deuteronomy 1:22). Moses allowed this, taking one man out of every tribe to form a reconnaissance team. This team brought back a divided report. Ten men decided the enemy was too strong to conquer and recommended Israel abort its attack. Two men believed that God would make a way for Israel's victory and recommended they proceed according to the word of the Lord through Moses. After weighing these conclusions, the people sided with the majority report and refused to follow Moses' command. Notice Moses' commentary on their behavior: "Notwithstanding ye would not go up, but rebelled against the commandment of the LORD your God" (Deuteronomy 1:26). He was careful to distinguish that their refusal to follow his orders was direct disobedience to God.

There is great freedom when followers "consider the source," accepting their leader as God's representative, and begin to follow that leader as unto the Lord. "Servants, be obedient to them that are your masters according to the flesh, with fear and trembling, in singleness of your heart, as unto Christ" (Ephesians 6:5).

Construct by Sowing

"These six things doth the LORD hate: yea, seven are an abomination unto him: a proud look, a lying tongue, and hands that shed innocent blood, an heart that deviseth wicked imaginations, feet that be swift in running to mischief, a false witness that speaketh lies, and he that soweth discord among brethren" (Proverbs 6:16-19). The sowing was anything but constructive in the camp of the Israelites. The people murmured in their tents, saying, "Because the LORD hated us, he hath brought us forth out of the land of Egypt, to deliver us into the hand of the Amorites, to destroy us. Whither shall we go up? Our brethren have discouraged our heart, saying, The people is greater and taller than we; the cities are great and walled up to heaven; and moreover we have seen the sons of the Anakims there" (Deuteronomy 1:27-28). Did you notice the reason they gave for not obeying the word of the Lord? "Our brethren have discouraged our heart [. . .]." The murmuring and complaining, the sowing of discord, created such a negative spirit in the camp that the Israelites openly rebelled against God.

A follower should be encouraging others on the team to follow leadership. Murmuring or grumbling about the leader's plan is silent rebellion that becomes a stumbling block to the process of execution. When people begin to lose faith in the plan, they also lose momentum and the work of the Lord comes to a grinding halt.

There is a right way to register a concern—and a wrong way. The Israelites' murmuring "in tents" was clearly inappropriate. A follower is welcome to go through the right channels to express concern or try to influence a decision of the leader but, once a decision is made, a follower should support it—both openly and privately. Instead of sowing the seed of discord a follower should sow the seed of contentment. This will foster unity and encourage teamwork.

Confide in Strength

A real key to being a consistent follower is learning where to place your confidence. The Israelites placed their confidence in the flesh, shifting their focus from following God's plan to following human personalities.

This drove them off course and they were greatly disappointed with the results.

Even though a follower should follow leadership as unto the Lord, their confidence must be in God. Leaders will come and go, but God never changes. Becoming obstinate because of the report of others or becoming obsessed with the personality of the leader are two extremes that should be avoided. God has given us leaders whom we can respect, love, and follow, but our confidence must be in His strength. Then, when leadership changes or fails to fulfill our expectations, we can continue following the Lord and the new leadership He brings into our lives.

Cancel Suspicion

The children of Israel began to doubt the power of God. They had seen and experienced his marvelous works; the ten plagues in Egypt, the parting of the Red Sea, the powerful defeat of the Egyptian army, and his provision through the wilderness; yet, when they came to their promised destination, they "did not believe the Lord" (Deuteronomy 1:32). This suspicion in their heart kept them from following Moses into the Promised Land.

Like the children of Israel we too have seen the power of God. When your leader challenges you to take a step of faith, remember these past victories. Courageously step out by faith, enthusiastically supporting the work of the Lord, no matter how big or how small.

Contemplate Solutions

Moses delivered the bad news, "And the LORD heard the voice of your words, and was wroth, and sware, saying, surely there shall not one of these men of this evil generation see that good land, which I sware to give unto your fathers, [. . .] But as for you, turn you, and take your journey into the wilderness by the way of the Red sea" (Deuteronomy 1:34-35, 40).

The people, realizing they had been caught and stinging from God's pronounced punishment, decided they would change their mind and follow God's original order. While suiting up for battle, God spoke again to the people through Moses, "Go not up, neither fight; for I am not among you; lest ye be smitten before your enemies" (Deuteronomy 1:42). God had already changed the order; it was too late for them to avoid the chastening of God. However, hoping to create their own solution they ignored Moses again and carried forth the battle. They were soundly defeated that day and many lives were lost.

God has a plan for every life. Realize there is a progression—God has a future in store for you. There will be times of confusion, times of discouragement, and times of remorse. Be careful not to make a problem bigger by inventing your own solution; rather, be willing to go through the process to see the plan of God unfold. Even though the punishment of sending the Israelites into the wilderness was severe, there was also an element of mercy: the adults would never inhabit the Promised Land— their children were to have that privilege; however, God's plan was to allow the parents to raise these children and then die a natural death in the wilderness. Think of all the wives that lost their husbands and the children who lost their fathers in the battle that day because of their continued rebellion. All this could have been avoided if they would have been willing to learn from their mistake.

Isaiah 50:10-11 should be underscored in every Bible: "Who is among you that feareth the LORD, that obeyeth the voice of his servant, that walketh in darkness, and hath no light? Let him trust in the name of the LORD, and stay upon his God. Behold, all ye that kindle a fire, that compass yourselves about with sparks: walk in the light of your fire, and in the sparks that ye have kindled. This shall ye have of mine hand; ye shall lie down in sorrow."

> *Isaiah 50:10-11 should be underscored in every Bible.*

Henry Ford once said, "Failure is the opportunity to begin again more intelligently."[20] Sometimes we must humbly admit where we have made a mistake, accept the consequences of that mistake, and resolve in our hearts to be better because of the experience.

PART FOUR

The Power of Follow-through

CHAPTER SIXTEEN

Accountability—Know What Is Going On

In a perfect world, you only have to ask once . . . reality is quite another story. Wouldn't it be great if you could assign tasks to your team and have complete confidence that the job is as good as done?

A fellow who worked for me had a great response to anything we asked him to do. He always said, "Consider it done!" Unfortunately it didn't always get done—in fact; we eventually had to let him go. Another fellow more accurately expressed himself, "We can do this!" He meant just that—together we had the potential of getting things done.

Depending on the quality of your personnel, you will have to maintain some level of involvement in the process of carrying out the plan after it has been assigned. Every member of the team—including you—will need to have some measure of accountability. No one should work in a vacuum. You need to know that everyone is progressing correctly.

There are many reasons people fail to carry out their assignments; primarily among them is that people honestly forget. The human capacity to remember what is said at meetings is many times limited by the notes your people take and keep accessible for further reference. This is especially true when you ask them to do something different from what they have been trained to do. You may have been there . . . you finish a meeting, feeling that you have communicated well, only to find out at the next meeting that no one can recall what was previously discussed. If they can answer the review questions at all, it is because they have scrambled for their notes!

Another problem is that people start out to do a task not really knowing how to complete it. Instead of looking for help, they will sometimes sit back and wait for help to come to them.Still others take on more responsibility than they can handle. Their intentions are good, but they can only accomplish so much at a time. People like this often work best alone and do not know how, or are not willing, to delegate any of their work to someone else.

There are other possibilities, but the result is the same. All of these problems hinder the accomplishment of the team's objectives. It takes a leader, working in concert with the team, to ensure the plan is carried through to the finish. It is not enough for the leader to just work alongside the team, although there is a time and place to do so. The involvement of the leader must be primarily strategic in nature, applying effort in areas that produce the greatest yield, all the while building accountability in the minds of the team members. In doing so you need to eliminate three areas: confusion, secrets, and surprises. Each of these will weaken the flow of information and impede accountability within the organization.

No Confusion

Keep good notes of the meetings. Be certain you know what work has been assigned to whom, and when the discussion took place. Do not leave to chance or memory what has been communicated. There is power in the printed page—have something in writing to which you can refer. Show your team that you intend for them to do what they have agreed to do by referring to your notes at each meeting, reviewing what has been assigned, and asking each person for an update on their progress. This is the best way to remind people of their duties; and in turn, avoids an awkward situation where you are forced to single out an individual who has failed to follow through with an assignment. This process of accountability becomes part of the agenda and motivates each team player to keep up to date with their responsibilities.

What you are trying to do is build a progressive motion. The Bible says, "For precept must be upon precept, precept upon precept; line upon line, line upon line; here a little, and there a little" (Isaiah 28:10). Once you solve a situation by developing a procedure and assigning someone to take responsibility, you should have documentation for the sake of clarity. This avoids having to solve the same situation twice. If it does resurface, you simply pull the file on that meeting, go back over the proper procedure, and remind the responsible person of their assignment. Furthermore, these notes will greatly help when replacements must be trained.

Due to the volume of information that will be exchanged in your team meetings, you will find yourself readily confused or unsure of what has taken place unless you take it upon yourself to keep good notes. Don't depend on a secretary to do all the paperwork. If you assign a secretary the responsibility of taking notes, double check the work and insist on accuracy. You need to know in certain terms what has been communicated. You will need a reliable record of what has been said to aid in the process of removing obstacles, which we will discuss in the next chapter.

A day or two after the meeting, it is an excellent idea to distribute a memorandum to all those present at the meeting, outlining what was discussed, assigned, and resolved. The tone can be one of thanks for their input and a reminder of the next appointed meeting.

However you decide to effect the transaction of information, be certain that there is an adequate paper trail. This helps keep your team moving forward—reminding them you are expecting to see action carried out on the team's decisions. Why keep meeting and re-meeting, assigning and re-assigning, solving and re-solving the same tired, worn-out issues. As we have learned from Isaiah 28:10, it may take a little time, but put the foundation in place correctly so that you will be in a position to move on to other issues—allowing the team to accomplish more.

No Secrets

A second area of importance: introduce a system of reporting or revise the current reporting if it is inadequate. You need a progress report as often as possible from each department that will give you an overall picture of the operation. Compare these reports with a week ago, a month ago, and last year. Is the organization growing or declining—are the objectives being reached? Look for trends as you determine if the team is making progress toward its goals.

Along these lines, have a system of checks and balances in place that allow you to verify the reports you receive. For instance ... the treasurer who accounts for the finances of the organization should give you his report and you should see the actual bank statements as well. Looking at the activity on the bank statements and viewing the canceled checks verifies that the report from the treasurer is an accurate and complete picture of the organization's financial condition. An important part of this system of checks and balances is to have all business mail come across your desk for review. If that is not possible, have at least two people reviewing it. Anyone receiving mail on behalf of the organization should welcome this shared responsibility, protecting the integrity of the organization and keeping you informed.

> *...have a system of checks and balances in place that allow you to verify the reports you receive. You need to lay your hands on the facts to keep the reporting diligent.*

It is impossible for a leader to verify every bit of information, especially as an organization grows. Obviously, you have to put a great deal of trust in the leaders with whom you surround yourself. However, it is wise to have the information available so you are able to look over their shoulder from time to time—your people never really knowing what you verify and what you don't.

There are many different motivations for people not completely squaring with you about how things really are. They range from not wanting to disappoint you, fear of losing their job, dishonest dealings, to even protecting people under them. It could simply be that their standards are not as high as yours—what is acceptable to them may be completely unacceptable to you. Whatever the case, you need to lay your hands on the facts to keep the reporting diligent.

When I was over the operations department at the rental car company, there were many reports—some on a daily basis, but the most significant came on a weekly basis, due in my office the night before the weekly district manager's meeting. These reports covered the weekly store audits completed by the district managers. These audit reports were the focal point of our meeting because they revolved around each location's

presentation, profitability, progress, problems, and personnel. Although some of the audit was objective in nature (involving facts and figures supported by documentation) much of it was subjective, calling for their critique
of certain items involving appearance, attitude, and aptitude at each location. Their reports, being subject to prejudice in varying degrees, were safeguarded by my physical inspection and random audits of each location. My findings were then compared to the district manager's findings, thus enabling me to ensure the quality of the information furnished.

The district managers grew to appreciate the accountability in the system explaining that it gave them support in the field as they dealt with their employees. Instead of having to be the "final arbiter"; responsibility for what they required was placed on someone who did not have to relate to the employees as closely or as often. This kept their relationship with the location manager positive and more productive, while accomplishing our objectives. Further, this ensured my information was accurate and current.

No Surprises

Hand in hand with a verifiable reporting system, put in a policy of "No Surprises!" among your team leaders. As leaders, they are responsible for keeping you fully informed. It is far better to know the truth—even if it is not what you want to hear—than to get caught by surprise. To make wise choices a leader must stay informed, knowing the best and worst about the organization and its team members.

As alluded to in the story above, you need to stop by and see your people while they are hard at work. Not only does this keep you informed, but sometimes this is a great encouragement to the team players who are getting the job done. Some folks could humorously be compared to a leaky bicycle tire. Occasionally they need to be pumped up. If they have enough air (encouragement) in them they will roll along just fine, but if they lose air pressure it is hard to get anything out of them. Many times a word of encouragement from the leader will strengthen them and lift their spirits. People love to know they are appreciated. Try to notice what they are doing correctly and comment on it! If you don't see anything in particular, or decide not to be specific, just a "Thanks for the job you are doing," or "We really appreciate your work" can go a long way toward boosting morale. Don't wait until they perform perfectly to encourage them. As long as they are on the team, do your best to make them feel a part of its success.

I remember being at a location, talking to the manager when my cell phone rang. The president of the company had some questions about the operations department. After we discussed business, he asked to speak to the location manager. I handed the phone over and could overhear the words being spoken, "I just wanted to tell you how much we appreciate the job you are doing out there." A few more sentences of cordial conversation was exchanged before the phone was hung up. The manager was beaming as he exclaimed, "That is why I work here!" Production at that location went through the roof that week.

> *It is your job as the leader to meet people where they are and develop them until they have reached their full potential...*

While you are out on the job, look for the bottlenecks. You may need to recruit more help or reassign responsibilities. You may find you are moving too fast or requiring too much. You may not be meeting often enough—some people work best when assigned one project at a time. Be objective and open to change as you move throughout your organization. Try to feel the rhythm, the heartbeat of the team. It is your job as the leader to meet people where they are and develop them until they have reached their full potential—maximizing their effectiveness for the sake of the goal being reached.

Whatever you discover, take time to do things right the first time. The hardest thing in the world to correct is a disaster after-the-fact. It is far easier to build what you've designed than it is to remodel what you inherit. People are creatures of habit—make sure they get into the right habits as you follow through with your plan.

~ ~ ~

Great materials, a brilliant design, ingenious manufacturing, and a huge parade at the launch does not mean you have a trustworthy ship. Will she stand up to the demands of the ocean? So many variables . . . the crew, the captain, the weather . . . all decide her fate. Likewise, follow-through will determine how effective you will be.

~ ~ ~

Are you organized, or will you agonize?

CHAPTER SEVENTEEN

Approaching an Obstacle

Much of our attention has focused on the steward of Luke 16, but for now we will turn the spotlight on the owner. Do you remember his situation? His top brass was accused of ugly tarnish: "There was a certain rich man, which had a steward; and the same was accused unto him that he had wasted his goods" (Luke 16:1). It seems that people under this steward were giving the owner troubling reports. The owner must have asked himself, "Could it be true that my most trusted man is selling me down the river . . .?" With disbelief in his heart, quite upset over what he had heard, he called a hurried meeting with the steward. He started out with a strong reprimand, "How is it that I hear this of thee?" He then demands a full audit, unloading a bombshell by threatening the steward with dismissal, depending on the findings of the audit: "Give an account of thy stewardship; for thou mayest be no longer steward" (Luke 16:2).

There are several things to gather from this account. Evidently, the owner did not know what was going on within his organization as covered in the previous chapter. If he had to demand an audit, it is possible he did not have access to evidence that would substantiate reports he had been receiving, if he had indeed been receiving any reports at all. Due to the surprise that seems to characterize this record, there may have been no system of accountability at all. The owner may have had blind faith in his steward.

Another point of interest: the owner did not take time to gather all the facts before calling the meeting. Because of this, the owner put himself in a position that would be analogous of a police officer pulling his weapon and aiming at a suspect without enough basis to pull the trigger. In fact, in this case, the owner had not even loaded his weapon! He made a huge accusation, threatening his top officer with dismissal, without evidence needed to come to a final decision. Revealing his hand, then leaving the matter hanging in the balance, unleashed a chain of events that certainly did not "tip the scales" in his favor.

> *One of the toughest things you will face as a leader is dealing with problems like the one presented in Luke 16.*

One of the toughest things you will face as a leader is dealing with problems like the one presented in Luke 16. Although *removing obstacles* will involve solving problems outside of the organization, which obstruct the pathway of the team; unfortunately, more often *removing obstacles* will involve dealing with people within your team who are hindering your progress. Dr. Bob Kelley, an experienced pastor, once said during a message, "Ninety-nine percent of all church trouble you have anytime or anywhere is not caused by the sinners without, it is caused by the saints within. I like what Dr. Vance Havner said, 'I'm not half as scared of the woodpeckers without as I am the termites within.' And brother he's exactly right."[21] It is a heartbreaking reality that you will have to deal with personnel problems—ometimes involving the most unlikely team members. Along these lines, there are three mistakes that will definitely break a leader:

Not Handling Enough Problems—This type of leader pretends everything is all right and hopes that if anything does happen to go wrong, perhaps with time it will magically correct itself. A leader like this either lives in a dreamworld with his head buried in the sand, or a world of fear fettered by followers who hold him hostage.

Handling Too Many Problems—Just as dangerous as handling too few problems is to over-react and handle problems that should be left alone or left to someone else's disposal. This leader, in an effort to stay informed becomes minutely involved in routine business, or expects more out of people than they can deliver.

Handling Problems at the Wrong Time – Unlike the leaders above, this leader may choose his battles carefully, but still loses conflicts by firing his shots before everything is in place and ready. The owner mentioned in Luke 16 exemplified this. He handled a valid issue, but his timing caused unnecessary disturbance and upheaval.

Nevertheless, obstacles will have to be approached and cleared if your team is going to progress with your plan; however, before you initiate the process, it is important to be prepared. A leader must exercise wisdom to know which obstacles to confront and exactly the right time and way in which to do so. From the situation between the steward and the owner, we draw several principles to guide us through this difficult process:

Investigate

Once you have been alerted to a possible problem, you must gather all the facts. Before approaching a team member, you need to know that you really have a problem. This sounds elementary, but it seems the owner of our story neglected this principle as he hurriedly convened a meeting. Listen to the wisdom of King Solomon, "[. . .] the honour of kings is to search out a matter" (Proverbs 25:2b).

This is one of the reasons a system of checks and balances is so important for every position. The owner may have had no choice but to go to the steward to collect information. This put him at a great disadvantage when accusations were made that had to be investigated. Accessible information allows you to investigate any team member without alerting that person that they are under suspicion.

When certain lines of trust are crossed, it is next to impossible to ever go back to square one. You never want to make accusations or even shed negative light on a team member unless you have adequate facts to support your suspicion. Once a subordinate is made aware that you are suspicious of him, the working relationship is likely to change. If the accusations are wrong, you may lose a working relationship that is advantageous to you and the team's objectives.

As a leader, you will hear many accusations. "If a ruler hearken to lies, all his servants are wicked," according to Proverbs 29:12. It is amazing but true—every crowd has at least one person who always seems to see the dark side of an issue. Everything seems negative and you rarely hear a positive report from this person. Sometimes a negative person's report is correct, so you can't ignore him, but you must investigate before acting on his possibly biased information.

Another consideration is that people may try to involve you as the leader in their personal battle with a co-worker. They try to pit you against their competitor by overemphasizing negative traits that may have an element of truth, but normally would be overlooked. If a person like this is able to get you "on their bandwagon," it will help him to gain leverage against a rival, but may cost you a good team member.

Often, things are simply not what they seem. The key in every situation: *don't jump to conclusions!* Take time to thoroughly investigate and gather information from several sources so you can form an unbiased opinion based on factual information.

Determine Their Motivation

Once you have investigated and found that an actual problem exists, try to determine the motivation behind this person's behavior. Why is this person acting this way? What is causing him to be unhappy? Before you have a meeting with a person who is causing a problem, it helps to have insight into his reasoning. The purpose is to determine if something can be done on your end that will solve the problem and change his behavior. Sometimes the team member is responding to issues over which you have control that could be changed without involving the person who is causing the problem. Other times, the problem is with that person and will necessitate their cooperation for its resolution. Whatever the case, when the motivation is discovered and removed, chances are the obstacle will dissipate and business will return to normal. Probe a little and try to find answers to the following questions:

- ***Has this person been treated fairly by the organization?*** It is quite possible that there has been an oversight that has caused him to feel unappreciated and is responsible for his poor attitude and lack of cooperation. We once had a situation where this was the source of our problem with an employee. Upon taking over the operations department of the rental car company, I inherited several problems. Among these, there were two location managers who had been allowed to drive company cars. Of course, the other managers wanted to know why they were not allowed the same benefit. Unable to provide a car for all managers, we corrected the problem by revoking the car privilege of these two managers, offsetting their loss of benefit with a generous raise in salary. One of the managers seemed pleased with the trade. For the other, I assigned his district manager to talk with him and handle the necessary arrangements. The district manager must have misunderstood my directive and neglected to award the raise, but did take away the benefit of the car. I asked the district manager for a report and was informed that everything had been handled. Three or four months later, we started having serious problems with the same location manager. He had been one of the finest managers in the company, but he was now one of the worst. I began investigating, trying to determine the motivation behind his problem. I discovered that he had never been given the allotted raise—no wonder he was so upset and uncooperative!

- *Has the organization provided adequate training for this person?*
- *Has this person been asked to handle a responsibility for which he is unqualified or incapable of performing—is he in over his head?* Everyone is not suitable for every position. This truth is expressed in Scripture, "For three things the earth is disquieted, and for four which it cannot bear: For a servant when he reigneth [. . .]" (Proverbs 30:21-22).
- *Does this person need help—is he overworked?*
- *Does this person have a problem at home that may be temporarily hindering his work?* Otherwise tremendous workers sometimes struggle with issues in their private life that causes them to falter in their public responsibilities.
- *What is this team member's track record*—is this an isolated incident?
- *Does this person respect structure*—are they generally a team player?

If you can find answers to these questions, you will be better equipped to handle the problems you've found with wisdom and understanding. "Through wisdom is an house builded; and by understanding it is established" (Proverbs 24:3).

Never React; Act

"He that is slow to wrath is of great understanding: but he that is hasty of spirit exalteth folly" (Proverbs 14:29). Now that you have a clear picture of the problem and have taken time to gain insight into why the problem developed, you need to create a strategy to solve the problem and remove the obstacle.

It is important that when you act, you do exactly the right thing at exactly the right time. The future of your organization will be impacted by the way you the problems that come your way.

After gathering the facts, a normal reaction is emotional in nature and not usually governed by sound wisdom. Put some time between your discovery of the problem and your action to solve it, in order to think things through. It is a good rule of thumb to never handle a problem the same day it is discovered. Take a night to sleep on it. If it is a major problem, or extremely emotional, give yourself a weekend or several weeks before settling in on a course of action. This delay gives you time to sort through the emotions and be certain you are responding with facts calculated to help the bottom-line of the organization.

> *It is a good rule of thumb to never handle a problem the same day it is discovered.*

For instance, let's say you are a manager of a retail store. It is close to Christmas and business is extremely hectic. You give a cashier a thirty-minute lunch break and she comes back an hour late. While she is gone, you have dealt with angry, frustrated customers because of the lack of cashiers. When she returns, you ask her why she is late. She mumbles some excuse about traffic and you know that she is evading the truth. Because of the trouble she has caused, your reaction would be to fire her on the spot with a remark like this, "If this is the best you can do, we don't need your help anymore; just go on home!" The problem is, you will then be short-handed the rest of the busy season. Chances are, you will not be able to hire and train a replacement quickly enough to be of any help and you will be stuck running a register, plus keeping up with your other duties.

The Bible says, "A fool uttereth all his mind: but a wise man keepeth it in till afterwards" (Proverbs 29:11). When you find out who is causing a problem; you are well on your way toward a solution. However, when and how you handle this information will determine how successful the team is. In the scenario of the cashier, you could document the incident, and then handle the problem after the holiday rush. In the meantime, a simple "Don't let that happen again" comment might be enough to keep her dependable during the time you need her most.

Don't Overreact

When you have investigated, determined motivation, and resisted the temptation to react, at some point you will be ready to act. Just a word of caution as you prepare: don't overreact. Use the least amount of pressure necessary to budge the obstacle. Why pull out a sledgehammer when just a light tap of a carpenter's hammer will do? You must resist the urge to call in the infantry and wage war on the person who has dared to upset the fragile balance of the smooth operation you have been conducting. Do you remember the old cartoon about the roadrunner and the coyote? They would blow up huge mountains and go to exaggerated extremes trying to get one another. Although we see this as humorous, we often do the same when confronted with problems that we have to handle.

It is impossible to get everyone functioning perfectly. You are an imperfect leader and you are dealing with imperfect people. You may have to overlook some things you don't like in order to accomplish the things that are really important. King Solomon had thousands of people working for him and he must have understood this principle well. Listen to his philosophy, "Also take no heed unto all words that are spoken; lest thou hear thy servant curse thee: For oftentimes also thine own heart knoweth that thou thyself likewise hast cursed others" (Ecclesiastes 7:21-22). He understood that if he insisted on perfection, he would not find anyone who could live up to that standard—even himself!

> *Why pull out a sledgehammer when just a light tap of a carpenter's hammer will do?*

Another observation of equal importance: just as it is impossible to get everyone functioning perfectly, you will find it equally impossible to get everyone functioning satisfactorily. You will have people who fulfill their responsibilities, but they have irritating characteristics like poor attitude, comment, taste, habit, preparation, etc. In certain positions these things may not really affect the overall team and its performance, but they may drive you crazy. The tendency is to become so focused on the idiosyncrasies of people that you forget the contributions they are making to the efforts of the team. When you start trying to change them, many times they will disappear, causing the team to lose a valuable player. What wisdom is expressed in Proverbs 14:4: "Where no oxen are, the crib is clean: but much increase is by the strength of the ox."

Even though some problems must be tolerated or overlooked, everything will not be that easy. There are issues that must be corrected if you are to protect the integrity of the team. The goal is to remove the obstacle and get the person back on the team, functioning in a way that contributes to the overall success of the objectives. Chapter nineteen discusses strategy for clearing these obstacles but, while still in the planning stage, develop a contingency plan. Size up the situation and plan what it will take to clear the obstacle from the path of the team. In other words, fire the smallest gun in your arsenal first while having a plan that would utilize the largest cannon you have, if needed to solve the problem.

In Conclusion

Try not to do any more damage to the working relationship than is absolutely necessary to solve the problem. If in your investigative step you discover a problem where the organization is at fault, then solve it, apologize if appropriate, and see if they improve. This may avoid having to discuss what they were doing wrong altogether. To conclude the story about our oversight of the employee's raise: once we discovered our error, we promptly called him in, apologized for the oversight, and gave him the intended raise—backdating it to make up the difference. We never had to discuss his behavior; when we solved our problem, it solved his problem and he returned to work satisfied.

Never forget, you need the people who follow you—they are the ones who will bring your plan into reality. They are replaceable, but it is better to deal correctly with the people you have than to be in a position of having to start over again, building a new team. The new team members may not have the same problems but, rest assured, they will have a whole new set. At least, with the people you have, you know pretty much what to expect after the problems begin to surface. Do your homework and approach the obstacles with confidence and precision.

CHAPTER EIGHTEEN

Receiving Instruction

Let's take a look at the previous chapter from the perspective of a follower. Perhaps you may be thinking that a leader in your past should have read what you've just read before approaching you. You can still remember how frustrated you felt being caught in the middle of circumstances that seemed so unfair. As far as you could tell, the leader had not done his homework; he never tried to see things from your standpoint or even listen to your reasoning; he reacted to the situation; and in your opinion, definitely over-reacted. In the heat of the moment, you were so angry that you had wished you could fire back an angry remark; and maybe you did, verbally or by your ensuing actions. Now, looking back with perspective, you realize that your response closed the door on an otherwise bright future with that organization. With a twinge of remorse, you wish that you now had another opportunity to relive that experience; however, you feel in your heart that even if you could go back in time, you would be helpless to do anything different.

You are not alone . . . almost everyone has faced a similar situation. It is difficult to accept negative feedback from someone in leadership, even when his or her approach is considerate and appropriate; on the other hand, it is incredibly frustrating to absorb the onslaught of a leader whose actions seem to be high-handed and overbearing. Remember the steward? You can almost feel his panic as the narrative unfolds: "And he [the owner] called him, and said unto him, how is it that I hear this of thee? Give an account of thy stewardship; for thou mayest be no longer steward. Then the steward said within himself, what shall I do? For my lord taketh away from me the stewardship: I cannot dig; to beg I am ashamed" (Luke 16:2-3). We have no idea what the steward's verbal response was to the owner's strong statements, but we do know that the resulting actions of the steward devastated his relationship with the owner, leading us to believe that he did not receive the instruction well. Suppose the steward's response would have been different? Maybe there would have been some opportunity for negotiation, regardless of the audit; however, the steward sealed his fate with his uncooperative reaction.

> ...it is incredibly frustrating to absorb the onslaught of a leader whose actions seem to be high-handed and overbearing.

The story of Daniel, in the Bible, is a fascinating example of a man who mastered the art of receiving instruction from leadership that God had placed over him. During his career, he served eight different Gentile kings and always emerged successfully each time he was in a confrontation. At one point in Daniel's career there is an excellent contrast, which provides great insight for us into this complicated issue of receiving instruction; but before examining this, we need to be reminded of Daniel's life.

Daniel was born and reared in Jerusalem during the great spiritual awakening under King Josiah. Following the king's death, his sons, Jehoahaz and Jehoiakim, departed from God and the forewarned, but prolonged judgment of God fell swiftly upon His people. At the young age of about sixteen, Daniel found himself a captive of King Nebuchadnezzar being deported to Babylon. Once there he was selected for government service, pressed into training, and given a Babylonian name, Belteshazzar. Although he was encouraged to turn his back on God in that heathen environment, time and time again he stood pure and true. In fact, nothing negative was ever written about Daniel throughout the Word of God.

His life is characterized by Daniel 6:4: "Then the presidents and princes sought to find occasion against Daniel concerning the kingdom; but they could find none occasion nor fault; forasmuch as he was faithful, neither was there any error or fault found in him."

In Nebuchadnezzar's kingdom, Daniel was promoted to great heights, but he remained loyal, humble, and pliable in the hands of a far greater King, Jehovah God. His character in the midst of paganism and plunder is a sight to behold; but becomes secondary, as one looks deeper into the twelve chapters of the book that bears his name. At a time when many would have been bitter and uncooperative, Daniel saw the divine hand of God at work, and availed himself of God's appointment to be His prophetic mouthpiece – declaring God's present and eternal purpose for the Jewish people. This included foreknowledge of the Gentile succession in power, right up through the great tribulation, which is yet to come. Daniel even predicted the coming of the Lord Jesus Christ to the earth, gave the time of His crucifixion, and predicted His future millennial reign on this earth.

Daniel was truly "a man greatly beloved" (Daniel 10:11) by God. Even our Lord Jesus spoke of him while on this earth (Mark 13:14). His wisdom and tenacity in the face of adversity was demonstrated early during his career when God revealed to him the dream of King Nebuchadnezzar and its interpretation. From some of the highlights of this story, told in its entirety in Daniel 2, we find great help to handle the high-handed and overbearing.

King Nebuchadnezzar had a dream that troubled him deeply. Believing there to be some significance to his dream, he called his wise men together and demanded them to interpret the meaning of his dream; but he would not tell them what the dream was. The wise men respectfully asked the king to tell them what he had dreamed and then they would give him the interpretation. Notice the demeanor of the king in his response to them, "The thing is gone from me: if ye will not make known unto me the dream, with the interpretation thereof, ye shall be cut in pieces, and your houses shall be made a dunghill" (Daniel 2:5).

The wise men again told the king that he would need to tell them what he had dreamed in order for them to be able to comply with his orders and interpret the dream. The king angrily responds, "I know of certainty that ye would gain the time, because ye see the thing is gone from me. But if ye will not make known unto me the dream, there is but one decree for you: for ye have prepared lying and corrupt words to speak before me, till the time be changed: therefore tell me the dream, and I shall know that ye can shew me the interpretation thereof" (Daniel 2:8-9).

Commentators are divided on exactly what should be inferred from Nebuchadnezzar's statement, "The thing is gone from me" (verses 5 and 8). Some think that he could not recall the specifics of the dream or that he had forgotten the dream completely. Others, like Dr. Lehman Strauss, believe that the king remembered the dream and was intentionally testing these wise men. Notice what Dr. Strauss has to say:

> Personally I do not believe that the king had forgotten the dream. My viewpoint is based upon verse 9 where Nebuchadnezzar says, "Tell me the dream, and I shall know that ye can shew me the interpretation thereof." How could the king know if their statement of the dream was correct unless he had remembered the dream? This tyrannical and unreasonable demand seems almost deliberate, as though he wanted to expose and ultimately dispose of these men who made pretense of having access to deep and hidden things. In further support of my view point on this matter I refer my readers to the more literal rendering of the statement, "The thing is gone from me" (verses 5 and 8). The Authorized Version has led some to the conclusion that the king was saying, "I have forgotten the thing (i.e., the dream)." But both Leupold and Young give their translation of the Hebrew. Leupold translates it, "The thing is certain with me" (page 60). There is little difference between the two [Leupold and Young]. Being in an ugly mood, the king is stating plainly that his demand is irrevocable. He had made up his mind and didn't intend to change it.[22]

Whether or not Nebuchadnezzar could remember the dream, it is clear to see that his demand was irrational and overbearing. After Daniel had revealed the dream and its meaning, the king even seemed to admit this to him: "Of a truth it is, that your God is a God of gods, and a Lord of kings, and a revealer of secrets, seeing thou couldest reveal this secret" (Daniel 2:47).

The wise men were sweating it out . . . they didn't know what to do. They were reeling from the punishment he had threatened; and all the while the king was growing more anxious and more demanding. Feeling caught in the grasp of an unreasonable leader, the Chaldeans, on behalf of the group, gathered their courage and rebuked the king: "There is not a man upon the earth that can shew the king's matter: therefore there is no king, lord, nor ruler, that asked such things at any magician, or astrologer, or Chaldean. And it is a rare thing that the king requireth, and there is none other that can shew it before the king, except the gods, whose dwelling is not with flesh" (Daniel 2:10-11).

This proved to be a dangerous maneuver on the part of these wise men. The Scripture records the outcome: "For this cause the king was angry and very furious, and commanded to destroy all the wise men of Babylon. And the decree went forth that the wise men should be slain; and they sought Daniel and his fellows to be slain" (Daniel 2:12-13).

It was that cut and dried. The king's orders would be carried out and hundreds would lose their lives. No one could stop his machine of twisted justice . . . well, that is no one but a young foreigner named Daniel. Notice what he did:

> Then Daniel answered with counsel and wisdom to Arioch the captain of the king's guard, which was gone forth to slay the wise men of Babylon: he answered and said to Arioch the king's captain, Why is the decree so hasty from the king? Then Arioch made the thing known to Daniel. Then Daniel went in, and desired of the king that he would give him time, and that he would shew the king the interpretation. Then Daniel went to his house, and made the thing known to Hananiah, Mishael, and Azariah, his companions: that they would desire mercies of the God of heaven concerning this secret; that Daniel and his fellows should not perish with the rest of the wise men of Babylon (Daniel 2:14-18).

> *With one simple request, an overbearing, unreasonable king was transformed into a workable, reasonable man who changed his mind and issued a stay of execution. What do you suppose made the difference?*

Can you believe what you have just read? With one simple request, an overbearing, unreasonable king was transformed into a workable, reasonable man who changed his mind and issued a stay of execution. What do you suppose made the difference? Let me suggest several things:

Daniel's Reputation Preceded Him

It is quite possible that the king had grown weary of the wise men's empty corruption; he certainly wasn't in a mood to negotiate with them in the least. There is no evidence that the king placed any value on the wise men he ordered destroyed. It seems clear that this was not the first time they had "crossed swords" with the king or his men.

On the other hand, Daniel and his friends had made an outstanding impression on Nebuchadnezzar: "And the king communed with them; and among them all was found none like Daniel, Hananiah, Mishael, and Azariah: therefore stood they before the king. And in all matters of wisdom and understanding, that the king inquired of them, he found them ten times better than all the magicians and astrologers that were in all his realm" (Daniel 1:19-20). The king knew these men were different and their entire lifestyle had commanded his respect.

When times are tight and circumstances have led you to a confrontation with your leader, it is too late to start working on your reputation—you can be assured it has already preceded you. The small choices you make on a consistent basis, even the things you feel are so insignificant, are added together into one great sum. This sum total determines the impression you have made and are making on the leadership above you. Proverbs 20:11 reminds us, "Even a child is known by his doings, whether his work be pure, and whether it be right." No wonder the Scripture says, "A good name is rather to be chosen than great riches, and loving favour rather than silver and gold" (Proverbs 22:1).

Daniel had a great reputation among the governing officials in Babylon, and it gave him audience when he and his friends needed special consideration. You will find that when you make yourself valuable to your leader, there will be much more concern and flexibility when it comes your time to receive instruction. Otherwise, you may find your leader indifferent and calloused, not really sure he is willing to make concessions to keep you on the team.

Daniel Remembered the Right Structure

A follower must always approach leadership with a strong remembrance of who is in charge. The wise men took upon themselves the privilege to argue with the king and "set him straight." Their brazenness earned them the punishment they deserved under the Babylonian system of justice. Daniel, in stark contrast, never argued with the command of the king nor did he demand anything.

Only those in authority have the right to command and instruct. A follower must be careful to remember that his basic responsibility is to heed and obey the orders of the leader whom God has placed over him. There is a process of appeal, which we will examine in Daniel's respectful communication, but structure must be maintained. This will demand, from time to time, for a follower to "swallow his pride" and do what the leader has asked him to do, without any argument.

Daniel Respectfully Communicated

There was nothing wrong with the wise men asking questions to try and clarify the instructions of the king, but they went too far when they assumed the role of leader and tried to convince the king that his command was unreasonable. Daniel, in much of the same manner had to gather the facts. He talked with one of the king's most trusted men, Aroich, to determine what was going on. It is apparent that Daniel had somehow missed the original meeting of the wise men and was shocked when he was summoned to his execution. He answered the summons with "counsel and wisdom" by posing this question, "Why is the decree so hasty from the king?" (Daniel 2:14-15). He did not reveal his emotions nor did he share his opinion, but he did open a line of communication to solve the puzzle of the hour: what is it that will satisfy the requirement of the king?

Daniel knew that the king must have been worried about something extremely important and it turned out that his dream was incredibly so, for it held the key to the future. Further, as a reasonable man, Daniel knew that the king would welcome a solution that relieved his problem, so he tuned in a listening ear and began to search for the right answer.

Daniel's wisdom and tact prepared the way for action that diffused the anger of the king and ultimately resolved the conflict. This respectful communication can be learned and incorporated into the life of a disciplined follower. James 3 gives us tremendous insight; outlining four practical steps of wise communication that will help you talk to your leader. To aid our memory, we will use the acrostic **T-A-L-K** as follows:

Talk Less – The first twelve verses of James 3 deal with the importance of controlling the tongue. Notice some of the highlights, "[. . .] If any man offend not in word, the same is a perfect man, and able also to bridle the whole body. [. . .] The tongue is a little member, and boasteth great things. Behold, how great a matter a little fire kindleth! [. . .] The tongue can no man tame; it is an unruly evil, full of deadly poison" (verses 2, 5, and 8). Saying too much to your leader is more likely to get you in trouble than not saying enough. The wise men said at least ninety-six words in response to the Nebuchadnezzar's instruction. This is in contrast to Daniel's brief request for a time extension.

Accept a Different Perspective – In other words, develop the art of being a good listener. A wise communicator never approaches conversation with a "know-it-all attitude," especially in the realm of talking with the leader. James 3:13 says, "Who is a wise man and endued with knowledge among you? Let him shew out of a good conversation his works with meekness of wisdom." A person who is truly intelligent realizes how limited his knowledge is, and he constantly opens his heart to a different perspective; all the while filtering what he receives through the bedrock of experience and sound reason. Communication involves vulnerability, a willingness to learn with an open mind that can readily adapt to a changing environment. The wise men emphatically ruled out the possibility of revealing the king's mysterious dream. His request went against their perception of logic, changed precedent, and redefined their job description. They were not even willing to identify with the problem of the king and take time to contemplate solutions. They dismissed his order as bizarre, whereas Daniel had the courage to entertain the idea of going beyond the established boundary and attempt what seemed unthinkable.

Look at the Facts – Refuse to deal on emotional ground. The wise men took the challenge of the king personally (it very well could have been) and moved quickly to defend their honor. However, matching wits with the greatest leader of their day did not exonerate their position. The emotions ran high, the words flew fast and thick, but the king closed the deal: "Destroy all the wise men of Babylon" (Daniel 2:12). There is so much regret on the part of all involved when things are said in the heat of a moment. Keep things on a higher plane – deal with the facts on an impersonal basis. James 3:14-16 says, "But if ye have bitter envying and strife in your hearts, glory not, and lie not against the truth. This wisdom descendeth not from above, but is earthly, sensual, devilish. For where envying and strife is, there is confusion and every evil work." Before losing control of your emotions follow Daniel's lead: respectfully ask for some time to think things over and see if you can get together with your leader again in the near future. It is rare when things have to be settled immediately. Give your leader and yourself some time to reflect on the meeting and hopefully refocus on the facts at hand. With this in mind, it should be pointed out that sometimes, like the wise men, the facts at hand involve you in a personal way. It is especially difficult to stay focused on the facts when you are being falsely accused. It is then that the advice of I Peter 2:18-20 is so helpful: "Servants, be subject to your masters with all fear; not only to the good and gentle, but also to the forward [perverse or crooked[23]]. For this is thankworthy, if a man for conscience toward God endure grief, suffering wrongfully. For what glory is it, if, when ye be buffeted for your faults, ye shall take it patiently? But if, when ye do well, and suffer for it, ye take it patiently, this is acceptable with God."

Keep Working Toward Solutions – If you use your imagination, there are innovative solutions just begging to be put in use. James 3 concludes: "But the wisdom that is from above is first pure, then peaceable, gentle, and easy to be intreated, full of mercy and good fruits, without partiality, and without hypocrisy. And the fruit of righteousness is sown in peace of them that make peace." Negotiate for peace by finding a way to complement the desire of your leader, joining with the agenda he has set, if at all possible.

Daniel Reasonably Appealed

The wise men sought to change the mind of their autocratic ruler and their appeal fell on deaf ears. Daniel, without any more answers for the king, came up with a reasonable appeal that saved all of their lives. Realizing that the king would not change his mind about the order he had given, Daniel asked him for more time, promising that he would show the king the interpretation of the dream. Daniel really had nothing to lose at that point. He had no guarantee that God would intervene on their behalf, but he was trusting that time would help to bring some solution to light. Daniel's appeal appeased the king's anger and he settled in to wait, hoping that Daniel would come through with a meaningful interpretation for his troubling dream.

Daniel left the presence of that earthly king and assembled a prayer meeting to talk to the King of Kings. Notice the nature of their request: "That they would desire mercies of the God of heaven concerning this secret; that Daniel and his fellows should not perish with the rest of the wise men of Babylon" (Daniel 2:18). They did not pray for God to change the king's mind, although I am not certain that it would have been wrong to do so. Instead, they prayed that God would change them – that God would give them wisdom and might to meet the demands of the king.

Maybe we ought to do more praying like this when we are faced with difficult situations. Maybe there is something that God can change in our lives that will allow us to be the followers we ought to be. Maybe the demands of your leader are overbearing, but are the powers of God limited? Can't God handle the highhanded? Instead of asking God to change everything in your life to make it easier, why not ask God to give you more grace and strength to be able to handle the load he has called you to bear.

Of course, an obvious difference should be pointed out and discussed. Daniel was enslaved in Babylon under the absolute rule of a king. He had no way out—that is true, but he still had the courage to pray for a solution to the king's dilemma instead of praying that God would show the king how unreasonable he was being. Still, there is a time when we should draw the line—a time to determine that there is no chance of working with the leader. There does come a time when a follower should quietly resign and find another place to serve, but this should be only after all the above negotiations have failed to bring remedy or when the leader has demanded something against God and will not reconsider.

Daniel Redeemed His Opportunity

After God revealed the dream to him, Daniel obtained an audience with the king through Arioch, promising him that he would interpret the dream. Arioch introduced Daniel, making this announcement to the king, "I have found a man of the captives of Judah, that will make known unto the king the interpretation" (Daniel 2:25). This peeked the king's interest and opened a grand opportunity for Daniel. Before Daniel revealed the dream, notice what he said:

> The secret which the king hath demanded cannot the wise men, the astrologers, the magicians, the soothsayers, shew unto the king; but there is a God in heaven that revealeth secrets, and maketh known to the king Nebuchadnezzar what shall be in the latter days. Thy dream, and the visions of thy head upon thy bed, are these; as for thee, O king, thy thoughts came into thy mind upon thy bed, what should come to pass hereafter: and he that revealeth secrets maketh known to thee what shall come to pass. But as for me, this secret is not revealed to me for any wisdom that I have more than any living, but for their sakes that shall make known the interpretation to the king, and that thou mightest know the thoughts of thy heart (Daniel 2:27-30).

What powerful words, all one hundred, thirty-six of them! Daniel went on to reveal the dream and interpret the meaning while the king eagerly listened. When Daniel finished speaking "Nebuchadnezzar fell upon his face, and worshipped Daniel, and commanded that they should offer an oblation and sweet odours unto him. The king answered unto Daniel, and said, Of a truth it is, that your God is a God of gods, and a Lord of kings, and a revealer of secrets, seeing thou couldest reveal this secret" (Daniel 2:46-47).

It is interesting to notice that what Daniel said to the king did not differ much from what the wise men had told him earlier; if anything it was more direct. Daniel was not afraid to stand up to the king, but he did so at the right time and in the right way. This brought about reconciliation instead of strife.

> *Instead of placing yourself in a win or lose conflict, why not go along with what the leader has requested, within reason, and let him see for himself the futility of his plan.*

What a powerful example for followers. All leaders will give instructions at some point that they will think better of later. Instead of placing yourself in a win or lose conflict, why not go along with what the leader has requested, within reason, and let him see for himself the futility of his plan. At some point, he will probably be willing to listen to what you have to say and will thank-you for your insight. Your timing and attitude will make the difference between your counsel being received or resented. For Daniel, his attitude and timing was backed up with solid answers to the king's quandary, and because of this he was promoted.

In Conclusion

Daniel had a reputation that preceded him, he respected the structure of the Babylonian system, he respectfully communicated with leadership, he reasonably appealed to authority, and he redeemed his opportunity to be heard. These things helped Daniel turn an extremely negative situation into a wonderful stepping-stone for his career so that God's cause could be advanced.

CHAPTER NINETEEN

Clearing an Obstacle

One of the most delicate things a person in leadership will ever do is confront a team member who has become an obstacle. The way this is handled will prove to impact the future of the organization in a positive or negative way. This chapter focuses on helping the leader of an organization think through the difficult process of dealing with this complex situation. Although specifically addressed to the leader, understanding this information will be of help to leaders and followers under this position; for if the leader's action to clear an obstacle is successful, it will be dependent upon their support.

A definition of terms should be made clear. Clearing an obstacle doesn't necessarily mean removing a person. The goal in removing an obstacle is to salvage the person creating the problem, thereby clearing the way for progress of the team's objectives. With the correct approach discussed in chapter seventeen, this goal can often be realized.

However, the only way to clear some obstacles is to remove a person who is at the root of the problem. The team as a whole must be considered and one person should not stand in the way of everyone's progress. As a general rule, team members should be given the opportunity to place themselves more firmly behind leadership through the process outlined in this chapter. At times, even after this opportunity is given, some people will refuse to be a team player and will not cooperate with the program. This leaves little choice but to move them along their way.

Before enacting the suggested steps within this chapter, a leader should ask himself this question: "What would it cost the team to lose this person right now?" The leader's efforts to clear an obstacle should be timed wisely so that any transition that becomes necessary will be made after there has been time for adequate preparation. Proverbs 12:9 gives this insight, "He that is despised, and hath a servant, is better than he that honoureth himself, and lacketh bread." The statement was clear to the farmers of that day. It is better to finish the harvest, storing the grain safely in the barn, before you fire a worker who has been disrespectful and disruptive. In other words, it is quite possible to solve an immediate problem only to create a crisis for the organization, later on.

> *Before enacting the suggested steps within this chapter, a leader should ask himself this question: "What would it cost the team to lose this person right now?"*

Also, depending on the seriousness of the obstacle being dealt with, there may not be enough time to go through all these proposed steps. Like the owner of Luke 16, a leader's investigation may find a serious problem that demands swift action to protect the organization. If that is the case, a leader should not serve notice to the person who has become an obstacle and give them time to make things worse. When a serious problem is brought to the surface, a leader must be ready with decisive action that limits the opportunity for further damage. Certainly the owner of Luke 16 must have wished that he had moved more aggressively, not giving his steward a chance to create such heavy losses for his organization.

Before getting into the specific steps of clearing an obstacle, a principle should be set forth. If at all possible, a leader should handle these situations through the right chain of command. Of course, if the person directly reports to the leader, there is no choice but to handle the situation directly; however, if there is someone in a position between the leader and the person, they should approach the situation first and try to handle it without the leader's direct involvement. A team member can work his way up, but once at the top he has no other recourse, but to resign or cause a larger problem if he feels that he has been handled unfairly. A follower should be given as many options as possible by making a meeting between the leader and this person a last resort.

It is a good idea for a leader to observe this principle even when handling minor situations. When the leader observes a problem, it will reinforce positional structure if the leader will make a mental note and have the person directly responsible for that area, solve the problem. A leader certainly has the right to go directly to any person under his leadership, but it is wise for the leader to allow the leaders under him to be the primary source of contact with their people.

Step One

The first effort to clear the obstacle should be a one-on-one meeting between the team member causing the problem, and the person directly responsible for that person's area, hereafter referred to as the "department head." After preparation is made according to the guidelines presented in chapter seventeen, the department head should meet with the team member in a casual, but business-like manner. The situation should be tactfully presented, allowing the team member the benefit of the doubt. No reprimand should be issued, but a careful explanation of the organization's expectations for that position should be reiterated. The department head should ask the team member if he understands what he is being asked to comply with. This will allow the team member an opportunity to question the purpose of the procedures. A careful explanation should be given for any concern the team member has and the department head should extend a sincere offer of help, reminding this person that the work is a team effort. They should be told something like, "We want to help you in order that you might be able to better help us, so that together we can be our very best." The department head should end this meeting on a positive note, confirming and encouraging the team member by reminding him that he is a valuable part of the success of the team and that the work he is doing is appreciated.

After this meeting, the department head should write a memorandum to the team member outlining what was discussed and decided with specific dates and times where appropriate. This should be delivered in person to the team member with the explanation that it serves as a reminder and record of the meeting that took place. There should be a place for the team member to sign and date the memorandum. It should be stated above his signature that the memorandum portrays an actual account of what was said and that he has received a copy. The department head should carbon copy (cc:) all the leaders above him, and file one copy as a permanent record. This begins a paper trail that documents the steps taken to clear the obstacle.

Many times this first meeting will clear the air and solve the problem. Misunderstandings are cleared up and the team member is refocused on his duties. Further, the written memorandum serves strong notice to the team member that the organization is serious about the issues that have been discussed, making this person accountable for what he has agreed to do.

Step Two

If the above meeting doesn't clear the path and the problem persists, a second meeting will have to be scheduled. This meeting should still be handled by the department head, but will have a different approach. The team member should be called in to the organization's headquarters, alerting him to the seriousness of the matter at hand and also bringing him out of his environment. The team member is then informed that there is still a problem. A copy of the memorandum should be referenced as the team member is reminded of the earlier meeting. The department head should attempt to ascertain what has hindered the team member from making the adjustments discussed in the previous meeting. Whatever his reasoning, the department head reminds him that the matter is not personal, but because he is responsible for that area, he simply must insist that the adjustments be made. The department head should then bring out a prepared, written directive that outlines a course of action to be taken. Where appropriate, an expected date should be given the team member regarding compliance. An offer of help should be extended again, and the meeting should end with the department head reminding the team member of his importance to the overall effort of the team. Once again, the team member should sign and date the directive, the leaders above should be carbon copied, and this directive should be filed in permanent record.

Step Three

If the problem persists, there is now a situation where a team member has ignored the request of his department head, both verbal and written. The next meeting is where the leader of the organization should get involved. The leader should call the team member in to meet with him and his department head. This meeting should not follow the course of the previous meetings. Remember, the leader needs to preserve the working relationship with this team member, if at all possible. The goal is to clear the obstacle that will bring this follower more firmly behind the structure of the organization.

The direct approach has already been used and has failed to bring this person around. The leader should use the fact that he has not met with this team member before, about the problem, to circle around and try a new approach. The leader is looking for common ground that will re-establish a workable structure. In doing so, he will try to avoid bringing up specific issues that will only treat the symptoms. Certainly by now, this person knows what they have been doing wrong and discussing what they already know will not solve the problem. Somewhere, this team member has gotten off course and it is the leader's job to try and refocus him, getting him back in line. The goal of this meeting is to dig deeply enough to expose and solve the root problem of the follower who has become an obstacle. Once this is solved, chances are the rest will fall into place under the supervision of the department head.

> *The goal of this meeting is to dig deeply enough to expose and solve the root problem of the follower who has become an obstacle.*

The leader should begin the meeting by thanking the team member for coming in. He proceeds by asking him how he is doing and how things are going with his responsibilities. The team member will probably not level with the leader in front of his department head, but the leader needs to give this person a chance to talk. (By the way, the leader should never let a team member by-pass the leadership under him to talk with him directly about a problem, or about the department head without that department head present. The team member will play one against the other and everyone will lose. A leader must support the leadership under him if he is going to build strong positional structure.)

After the team member has finished talking, the leader should start the discussion by commending this person for the things that he is doing well. If true, tell this team member that the department head has confidence in him and considers him to be a valuable part of the team. If the leader can build up the department head, it will help the team member respect and follow that person better. Further, the leader should try to mentally take the team member back to when he first joined the team, by reminding him of the accomplishments that he has been an integral part of. This effort impresses upon this person the mutual investment that has been made in the organization.

Using broad strokes, the leader should paint for him the big picture of the dreams and hopes of the team, emphasizing how important the role he plays will continue to be to the success of the team's objectives. The principles of the organization should be covered and the team member should be reminded of why these things have been put in place. The leader should communicate in a general way that there are certain things that have to be done to protect the integrity of the team and everyone must live up to their part. The leader should discuss the opportunities ahead that will benefit this person—things that he has to look forward to.

The leader is trying to restructure the attitude of this uncooperative team member so that he will look beyond the areas in which he is struggling. Hopefully, the reward will outweigh his reluctance and he will find it easier to pull his share of the load so the team can reach its goals. The leader is trying to rekindle his desire to make things work. At one time he must have been enthusiastic about his duties and the leader is trying to determine what it will take to bring him back to that place of cooperation.

Before ending the meeting, the leader should ask if there is anything they can help him with. After listening to his response, the meeting is closed by the leader telling him that he has a lot of confidence in his abilities and looks forward to working with him in the future.

Again, the meeting should be documented, signed by the department head and the leader, and added to the file. This record should be kept for accountability of the meeting and demonstrates the desire of the organization to work with the team member. It lends evidence that the leader has gone through all possible means to salvage the working relationship.

Step Four

If step three fails to clear the obstacle, there is no choice but to release the team member responsible for the on-going problem. The leader should call a meeting with the department head and the team member. At this point discussion is unnecessary and should be avoided. The leader simply says something like, "We are sorry things have not worked out. Thank-you for what you have done and we wish you well." The meeting should be kept professional and the tone should be kind. The leader and department head should resist the urge to tell the person how disappointed they are in him. The decision to let them go has already been made and remarks of this sort will only make things worse. If the team member asks why he is being let go, the response of the leadership should be confined to the written paperwork that has already been presented to him in the past. It may be a good idea for the leader to gently say, "Look, there is nothing personal, it just hasn't been a good fit. I'm sure things will work out better for you somewhere else." The leaders should extend their hands to this person and try to end the relationship on a good note - at least as far as the organization is concerned. If the team member gets angry and tries to argue, the leader and department head should refuse to get on that level. Once again, a discussion will not change the decision that has already been made. Time for discussion was during the meetings that were held prior to their discharge. Remember, the organization has been fair with this person and has given him every opportunity to do the right thing. He has made his choice to persist in compromising the integrity of the organization and the leadership has simply made a decision that protected the interests of everyone.

If the structure of the organization, does not allow the leader to release the individual, the leader must begin to work this person out of responsibility and start to assign his tasks to others. If this is the case, it still may prove beneficial for the leader to meet with the person and ask for his resignation. The merits of that decision will have to be weighed against the possible ramifications.

In Conclusion

If you are the leader of an organization and you lack the authority necessary to remove a major obstacle, there is a serious question, which should be posed to the positional structure. You may not have the right foundation to accomplish the plan and preparation of your heart. You may need to begin to look for another foundation, before pitting yourself in a conflict that holds no promise of victory. The other option is to wait until the Lord allows you to redesign the positional structure or providentially removes the obstacle that hinders the progress of the organization. The Lord may direct you to wait until He chooses to do this, or He may lead you on to a better foundation. Much could be said about this topic, but suffice it to say you must do some prayerful soul-searching about the direction of your life when faced with this type of dilemma. Before making any concrete decisions, seek Godly counsel and wisdom from someone you trust.

~ ~ ~

Growing up, I lived beside a farm. It was a wonderful old farm that was home to a recently widowed lady. I often did work around the farm and one of my jobs was to feed three mules and a horse every afternoon. One of the benefits of the job (I guess you could call it that) was permission to ride the mules or horse. I knew very little about riding, but had a grand time in spite of my inexperience—especially riding the horse. He was a tired, old mount that had become barn sour after his master passed away. I had to fight the horse every step of the way to get him to leave the barn; however, when I finally allowed the horse to go back to the barn, he would tear off at a dead gallop. The fight was then to try to get him stopped before he knocked my head off at the entrance to the barn.

It was even worse when I tried to ride one of the old mules. He would stand stock still when I tried to make him go, and lunge ahead when I finally gave up and was trying to dismount. I would then swing back into the saddle and hang on for dear life as the mule galloped around the paddock, trying to crush my feet into the fence. If the gate happened to be open, he would tear out across the pasture running under every low-hanging branch.

Needless to say, that horse and those mules worked me over. I don't think I ever really rode them, but they sure took me for a ride!

~ ~ ~

In like fashion, if you don't follow-through carefully with personnel problems, your followers may end up "working you over" and the organization will falter, if not fail. This holds true in working with volunteers or paid staff. Do you remember Jesus' commentary on the story of the unjust steward? "For the children of this world are in their generation wiser than the children of light" (Luke 16:8b). Secular organizations all over the world have cleared obstacles from their path by following steps similar to what has been outlined in this chapter. Why not use these same principles to deal with problems as we conduct a work for the Lord?

Harness the power of your team by maintaining strong leadership. Your team will respect your diligence and rally around a leader who will clear the obstacles with the correct approach and process.

CHAPTER TWENTY

The Future in Focus

After Jesus finished telling the fascinating story about the steward, do you remember the application He made to His disciples? "And I say unto you, Make to yourselves friends of the mammon of unrighteousness; that, when ye fail, they may receive you into everlasting habitations" (Luke 16:9). With Jesus' characteristic boldness, He jolted the disciples into focus by using a vivid reminder of their mortality – one day they would die and everything they had done for this world would fade away. Because of their faith in Jesus, the disciples had a home in Heaven to look forward to, but what about their friends, their loved ones, their community, and the rest of the world? Jesus was encouraging His disciples to use every earthly means available to reach their goal of winning the lost, motivated by a desire to see precious souls in Heaven for eternity.

As believers, we need to examine our priorities and the preparations that we are making for eternity. Jesus told the story of the unjust steward to bring the future in focus. Just as the steward made earthly preparation for future employment and success in the temporal world, believers should be making earthly preparation for eternity by using every possible means to further the cause of Christ. This work that we have been called to do changes the eternal destiny of souls—what could be more important?

> *Just as the steward made earthly preparation for future employment and success in the temporal world, believers should be making earthly preparation for eternity by using every possible means to further the cause of Christ.*

What if Billy Sunday, the great evangelist whose story was told briefly in chapter seven, had not caught the vision of carrying forth the gospel? What if his baseball career had been more important? Many thousands of people would have perished had he failed to prioritize the work of winning precious souls to Jesus. Thankfully, because of his concerted effort, hundreds of thousands formed a welcoming committee to greet Mr. Sunday as he stepped onto the golden streets of Heaven on November 6, 1935.

Every believer has been given the task of carrying forth the gospel, but many have never caught the vision. It is true, God doesn't call every believer to be an evangelist like Billy Sunday, but He has called every believer to be a preacher in the context of Mark 16:15, "Go ye into all the world, and preach the gospel to every creature." Every believer should take an active part in the effort of spreading the gospel. Think of the many who would be converted if more believers would surrender to this command.

More provoking still, some have surrendered, yet fail to be diligent in His work. Just like Jesus said long ago, the world continues to be wiser in reaching their temporal goals than we are in reaching our eternal one. Many believers show much greater wisdom in making preparation for their career, their family, their retirement, or things of this temporal world than they do in making preparation for eternity in Heaven. What a soul-searching thought! Why should the pursuit of business or pleasure be considered more important than reaching people for Christ? Further, why consider the principles of sound business only to be effective in building temporal business? Why not use all this ingenuity and technology to further the gospel of Christ?

Dear friend, please search your heart. Are you putting your effort into building the kingdom of God, or are you setting your sights on much less? If you graduated to Heaven tomorrow, who would be there to welcome you? Who else is on their way to Heaven, because of your witness? Will the things you are dreaming of and striving for now really matter when your mortal life is over and eternity begins?

The Apostle Paul, under the inspiration of the Holy Spirit, wrote to Timothy and gave him some excellent advice. Young Timothy had just become the director of a great missionary effort in the city of Ephesus. Paul encouraged him to bring the future in focus by establishing five prerequisites for his life. These same principles are applicable to any believer who desires to be wiser than the world. Notice Paul's instruction in I Timothy 6:6-14:

> **6** But godliness with contentment is great gain.
>
> **7** For we brought nothing into this world, and it is certain we can carry nothing out.
>
> **8** And having food and raiment let us be therewith content.
>
> **9** But they that will be rich fall into temptation and a snare, and into many foolish and hurtful lusts, which drown men in destruction and perdition.
>
> **10** For the love of money is the root of all evil: which while some coveted after, they have erred from the faith, and pierced themselves through with many sorrows.
>
> **11** But thou, O man of God, flee these things; and follow after righteousness, godliness, faith, love, patience, meekness.
>
> **12** Fight the good fight of faith, lay hold on eternal life, whereunto thou art also called, and hast professed a good profession before many witnesses.
>
> **13** I give thee charge in the sight of God, who quickeneth all things, and before Christ Jesus, who before Pontius Pilate witnessed a good confession;

14 That thou keep this commandment without spot, unrebukeable, until the appearing of our Lord Jesus Christ:

Flee

In order to bring the future in focus, you must "flee these things" (verse 11a). What things does this verse reference? From verses 6-10 it is clear that Paul was admonishing Timothy to flee from discontentment that would cause him to pursue worldly riches.

To be content is to be satisfied with God's provision through your labor. God approves of work. Earlier in this passage, Paul gave clear instruction for believers to earn provisions for their basic needs: "Let as many servants as are under the yoke count their own masters worthy of all honour, that the name of God and his doctrine be not blasphemed. And they that have believing masters, let them not despise them, because they are brethren; but rather do them service, because they are faithful and beloved, partakers of the benefit. These things teach and exhort" (I Timothy 6:1-2).

Unless you have been called to full-time Christian service, it is not wrong to work a secular job to earn money that will enable you to provide for your family; in fact that is God's plan. The question you should ask yourself is, "When is enough, enough?" Paul tempered his instruction to Timothy with this statement: "And having food and raiment, let us therewith be content" (verse 8).

When you are satisfied with God's provision through your labor, you can then put all your creativity, focus, and energy to work striving to build the Kingdom of Heaven. It is impossible to serve two masters. If money and the things of this world grip your affection, there is little room left for effective service for Christ. You must make a decision . . . will you focus on the things of this fleeting world or will you bring the future in focus?

Follow

Next, Paul admonished Timothy to "follow after righteousness, godliness, faith, love, patience, meekness" (verse 11b). Instead of pursuing the things of this world, a person with the future in focus will seek to establish and maintain his or her testimony of a changed life. This will enable

this person to be an effective witness for Christ. Paul listed specific characteristics that Timothy should concern himself with:
- Righteousness – having the right behavior.
- Godliness – having the right attitude.
- Faith – having a strong dependence upon God's strength.
- Love – having the love of Christ for others.
- Patience – having a willingness to wait on God's timing.
- Meekness – having strength under God's control.

Fight

"Fight the good fight of faith" (verse 12a). So many are willing to scale any height for the sake of worldly pursuit, but are so faint of heart when it comes to the work of God! How we need soldiers—real men and women of God who will defend the truth of salvation and valiantly carry the gospel at any cost. Certainly, as a believer you are aware of the spiritual warfare. Satan, God's archrival, seeks to defeat those who seriously go to work for God. You must make up your mind right at the start that this cause is worth fighting for. In Paul's second letter to Timothy, he gave him several qualities of a good soldier.

First of all, a soldier must be strong: "Thou therefore, my son, be strong in the grace that is in Christ Jesus" (II Timothy 2:1). Whereas a soldier needs physical strength; a soldier of the cross needs spiritual strength. This strength can be found by the power of the Holy Spirit working through your life.

Secondly, a soldier realizes the value of the team: "And the things that thou hast heard of me among many witnesses, the same commit thou to faithful men, who shall be able to teach others also" (II Timothy 2:2).

Thirdly, a soldier is willing to endure hardship: "Thou therefore endure hardness, as a good soldier of Jesus Christ" (II Timothy 2:3).

Finally, a soldier is committed: "No man that warreth entangleth himself with the affairs of this life; that he may please him who hath chosen him to be a soldier" (II Timothy 2:4).

All of these qualities have been exemplified many times over in the history of our great country. If we would be willing to be a good soldier and fight for our earthly country, how much more should we be willing to fight for our Heavenly country.

Focus

Think of the achievements for the kingdom of God that could be recognized if you were to concentrate all your effort. Paul put it this way, "Lay hold on eternal life, whereunto thou art also called, and hast professed a good profession before many witnesses. I give thee charge in the sight of God, who quickeneth all things, and before Christ Jesus, who before Pontius Pilate witnessed a good confession" (verses 12b-13).

Literally, set your affection on Heaven that you might carry forth the ministry of the Lord Jesus Christ. In John 18:37, Jesus gave testimony before Pilate about the purpose for His life, "To this end was I born, and for this cause came I into the world, that I should bear witness unto the truth." What greater purpose could there be in life, than to follow in the footsteps of Jesus?

Finish

Paul encouraged Timothy to finish strong: "That thou keep this commandment without spot, unrebukeable, until the appearing of our Lord Jesus Christ" (verse 14). Once you begin to serve the Lord, stay with it. Make up your mind from the outset that you will be faithful until Jesus comes again. Before Jesus ascended back to Heaven, He spoke these words: "Lo, I am with you alway, even unto the end of the world" (Matthew 28:20b). This was the favorite text of pioneer missionary to Africa, David Livingstone. At every crisis in his life he would write it in his diary and add: "It is the word of a Gentleman of the strictest and most sacred honor, and that's the end of it!"[24] God's special presence is with us as we seek to accomplish the great commission He has entrusted to our care.

> *Failure can be a great tool used of the Lord to help bring your future in sharp focus.*

There may be some failures along the way, but that is no excuse to abandon the mission. The steward of Luke 16 had a quality that is worth imitating: when he failed, he got up and went back to work. Al Neuharth, founder of USA Today, warns, "If you are over 30 and haven't had a major failure in your business or professional career, time is running out on you . . . It needs to be a big failure. You can only fail big if you take a big risk. The bigger you fail, the bigger you are likely to succeed later."[25] Failure can be a great tool used of the Lord to help bring your future in sharp focus. Be willing to learn from the mistakes of failure and determine to go forth again stronger and better equipped to succeed. Further, Don't let the failure of others bring down the final curtain on your performance. Regardless of what anyone else does, you must finish your course.

The truth is you will organize; there will be some focus for your life. Why not organize for the Master in His service? You may find temporal satisfaction while pursing earthly dreams, but these investments will not matter when eternity begins. Think of the many souls you could point to the Saviour. In the words of Billy Sunday, "Let's quit fiddling with religion and do something to bring the world to Christ."[26] Eternity is depending on your decision . . . will you

Organize or Agonize?

NOTES

1. Albert Barnes, *Notes on the New Testament Explanatory and Practical: Luke and John* (Grand Rapids: Baker Book House, 1974) 111.

2. "Follow," Def. 10 & 11, *Webster's New World Dictionary: of the American Language*, ed. David B. Guralnik, 2nd coll. ed. (New York: Prentice Hall Press, 1986).

3. "Eusplagchnos," Def. NT:2155, *Biblesoft's New Exhaustive Strong's Numbers and Concordance with Expanded Greek-Hebrew Dictionary*, 1994, PC *Study Bible for Windows*, Software, Vers. 3.0 (Biblesoft and International Bible Translators, Inc., Mar. 1999).

4. James Dobson, *Love is for a Lifetime* June 1988, "Marriage," Index 1620-21, *Bible Illustrator for Windows*, Software, Vers. 1.0d (FindEx.com, Inc., 1994).

5. "Marriage, Commended: Little Defects," Feb. 1987, Index 1620, *Bible Illustrator for Windows*.

6. "Jealousy, Human: Counting Your Ribs," Feb. 1986, Index 1851, *Bible Illustrator for Windows*.

7. "Hatred, Examples of," Index 2211, *Bible Illustrator for Windows*.

8. Millard J. Erickson, *Christian Theology*, 2nd ed. (Grand Rapids: Baker Books, 2000) 494.

9. "Creative Quotations from Billy Sunday (1862-1935)," *Electric Library*, 2000, "The Speaker's Electronic Reference Collection," Aapex Software, 1994, 12 Jan. 2001 <http://www.bemorecreative.com/one/193.htm>.

10. William T. Ellis, *"Billy" Sunday: The Man and His Message* (Philadelphia: John C. Winston, 1914) 31.

11. Ellis 41.

12. Ellis 15.

13. Ellis 328-30.

14. Ellis 158.

15. C. I. Scofield, ed., The Scofield Study Bible (New York: Oxford University Press, 1909) 956.

16 James Smith, *Handfuls on Purpose*, Ser. 9, (London: Pickering & Inglis, n.d.) 43.

17 "Parental Influence," Apr. 1988, Index 1632-33, *Bible Illustrator for Windows*.

18 "Dia," Def. NT:1223, Biblesoft's New Exhaustive Strong's Numbers and Concordance with Expanded Greek-Hebrew Dictionary, 1994, PC Study Bible for Windows.

19 "Hupomone," Def. NT:5281, *Biblesoft's New Exhaustive Strong's Numbers and Concordance with Expanded Greek-Hebrew Dictionary, 1994, PC Study Bible for Windows*.

20 "Failure: Spiritual," Index 4034, *Bible Illustrator for Windows*.

21 Bob Kelley, "What to Do When the Devil Gets in the Church," rec. 17 Apr. 1983, audiocassette, Franklin Road Baptist Church, Murfreesboro, TN.

22 Lehman Strauss, *The Prophecies of Daniel* (Neptune, New Jersey: Loizeaux Bro., 1969) 57.

23 "Skolios," Def. NT:4646, *Biblesoft's New Exhaustive Strong's Numbers and Concordance with Expanded Greek-Hebrew Dictionary, 1994, PC Study Bible for Windows*.

24 John Phillips, *Exploring Revelation* (Neptune, New Jersey: Loizeaux Bro., 1991) 24.

25 Kenneth O. Gangel, *Using Multiple Gifts to Build a Unified Vision: Team Leadership in Christian Ministry* (Chicago: Moody Press, 1997) 215.

26 Ellis 61.

BIBLIOGRAPHY

Barnes, Albert. *Notes on the New Testament Explanatory and Practical: Luke and John.* Grand Rapids: Baker Book House, 1974.

Bible Illustrator for Windows. Software, Vers. 1.0d. FindEx.com, 1994.

Biblesoft's New Exhaustive Strong's Numbers and Concordance with Expanded Greek-Hebrew Dictionary. 1994. *PC Study Bible for Windows.* Software, Vers. 3.0. Biblesoft and International Bible Translators, 1999.

Dobson, James. *Love is for a Lifetime.* N.p.:n.p., 1988.

Electric Library. "The Speaker's Electronic Reference Collection," Aapex Software, 1994. 12 Jan. 2001 <http://www.bemorecreative.com/one/ 193.htm>.

Ellis, William T. *"Billy" Sunday: The Man and His Message.* Philadelphia: John C. Winston, 1914.

Erickson, Millard J. *Christian Theology.* 2nd ed. Grand Rapids: Baker Books, 2000.

Gangel, Kenneth O. *Using Multiple Gifts to Build a Unified Vision: Team Leadership in Christian Ministry.* Chicago: Moody Press, 1997.

Guralnik, David B., ed. *Webster's New World Dictionary: of the American Language.* 2nd coll. ed. New York: Prentice Hall Press, 1986.

Kelley, Bob. "What to Do When the Devil Gets in the Church." rec. 17 Apr. 1983, audiocassette. Franklin Road Baptist Church, Murfreesboro, TN.

Phillips, John. *Exploring Revelation.* Neptune: Loizeaux, 1991.

Scofield, C. I., ed. *The Scofield Study Bible.* New York: Oxford University Press, 1909.

Smith, James. *Handfuls on Purpose.* Ser. 9. London: Pickering & Inglis, n.d.

Strauss, Lehman. *The Prophecies of Daniel.* Neptune: Loizeaux, 1969.